MacARTHUR AND THE WAR AGAINST JAPAN

MacARTHUR
AND THE
WAR AGAINST JAPAN

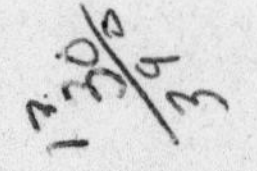

Books by Frazier Hunt

MacARTHUR AND THE WAR AGAINST JAPAN

BLOWN IN BY THE DRAFT

THE RISING TEMPER OF THE EAST

SYCAMORE BEND: *a novel*

CUSTER: THE LAST OF THE CAVALIERS

THE BACHELOR PRINCE

THIS BEWILDERED WORLD

ONE AMERICAN

THE LITTLE DOC

THE LONG TRAIL FROM TEXAS

MacARTHUR
AND THE
WAR AGAINST JAPAN

BY

FRAZIER HUNT

★★★★

NEW YORK
CHARLES SCRIBNER'S SONS
1944

Printed in the United States of America

A

THIS BOOK IS
MANUFACTURED UNDER WARTIME
CONDITIONS IN CONFORMITY WITH
ALL GOVERNMENT REGULATIONS
CONTROLLING THE USE OF PAPER
AND OTHER MATERIALS

To

JOHN J. PERSHING,

General of the Armies of the United States,
this volume is dedicated with affection
and gratitude.

GENERAL HEADQUARTERS
SOUTHWEST PACIFIC AREA
MILITARY INTELLIGENCE SECTION, GENERAL STAFF

18 May 1944

PREFACE

I FIRST MET FRAZIER HUNT MORE THAN TEN YEARS AGO WHEN I was an instructor at the Command and General Staff School at Fort Leavenworth, Kansas. He was visiting Army friends there and spent much of his time talking war with student officers and members of the faculty. He displayed an unusual grasp of military affairs. His thirst for military knowledge was eager—almost insatiable.

Frazier Hunt, as war correspondent, was at the front during four of the five major campaigns of World War I. After the War, he was the first American to see the great revolution in Russia. He has talked to Lenin and many of the early Red leaders. From the start, he predicted the Red Revolution would succeed. After he came out of Russia, he joined General Graves in the Far East.

Few writers have a greater understanding of the Orient than has Frazier Hunt. He was the first American to interview Gandhi. He knew Sun Yat-sen. He knows Chiang Kai-shek. His close friendship with Manuel Quezon began in the Philippines in 1920. He has known Admiral Togo and many other leading Admirals and Generals of Japan, including the soldier-priest, General Araki.

All his life, Frazier Hunt has searched for truth and human understanding. He has studied deeply the undersurface, revolutionary ferment among underprivileged people. The picture of our restless world and its great personalities which he has brought to American readers through his books, articles and radio talks represents the best in journalism.

Frazier Hunt has followed World War II from its genesis to the beaches of Hollandia. In 1940, he was an observer in the Middle East, then he saw the German war machine break the frontier and overrun the Low Countries. In January, 1944, he joined the Pacific Fleet and took part in the operations against the Marshalls.

He came to the Southwest Pacific area in February, 1944. Since coming here, he has had frequent and long talks covering every phase of the operations with officers who have lived the Pacific War from Bataan to Biak. He has had access to the historical data available at this Headquarters. His analyses of the campaigns are accurate.

His point of view, although frank and rugged, is always sincere. Frazier Hunt returns to America with the affection and respect of all those who have known him in this Command.

C. A. WILLOUGHBY,
Brigadier General, U.S. Army,
Chief, Mil. Intell. Section, General Staff,
G.H.Q., Southwest Pacific Area.

MacARTHUR
AND THE
WAR AGAINST JAPAN

CHAPTER ONE

It was around 7:30 on the Sunday morning of July 27, 1941, when General Douglas MacArthur sat down to his breakfast and the Manila *Tribune*.

His eyes caught a small box on the front page. It was a flash from Washington, and announced without confirmation that the Philippine Army was to be called to the colors under the command of a Lieutenant General. It was rousing news and very, very interesting to this retired four-star American General and Philippine Field Marshal.

The biggest front-page story, however, had to do with the Japanese occupation of Indo-China, and with the landing that day of 30,000 Japanese troops in Saigon. Some 1,900 Japanese army trucks were already there waiting for them. It meant that Japan had at last actually embarked on her drive of conquest and ruin; that she had at least temporarily by-passed the Philippines, and the token American forces there.

The two stories fitted together in the General's alert questioning mind. Washington had finally awakened to its peril and shifted for the moment its attention from the Atlantic to the more dangerous Pacific. If this Washington news flash were true, and the Philippine Army, that MacArthur had organized and trained and fathered, was to be called up, who would command it?

The doorbell of the General's pent house atop the Manila Hotel rang. The houseboy brought in a telegram. It was cryptic, but it made sense. It contained a single word: "Congratulations," and it was signed "Lehrbas"—an old newspaper friend who had covered the War Department when the General was Chief of Staff. Was that one word "Congratulations" the missing clue?

The bell rang again and two more messages were handed him. The General took down the phone and put in a call for Dick Sutherland, Chief of Staff of the Military Mission. Sutherland was not in his quarters, so he called for the Deputy Chief, Dick Marshall. Would Marshall locate Sutherland and the two come over to the Manila Hotel?

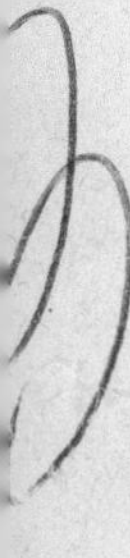

It was a little after ten o'clock when Sutherland and Marshall were ushered into the General's study. Quickly he read them the two telegrams that he had just received. One was an open message stating that the President of the United States had ordered the Philippine Army mobilized under the command of Douglas MacArthur. A strange feature of the action was his recall to active service in the rank of Major General, two grades below his retired American rank of General and three grades below his Philippine rank of Field Marshal. But he was to be at once promoted one grade to Lieutenant General. The other telegram ordered the formation of a new command, the United States Army Forces in the Far East, under MacArthur. He was to have full authority, and was authorized to spend ten million dollars to cover the initial expenses of mobilization and preparation.

MacArthur had barely finished reading the two dispatches when a phone call from Malacanan Palace informed him that President Quezon was on his way to the hotel. The General and his two senior assistants reached the hotel entrance just as the President's car drove up. The President, his bright eyes shining, impulsively put his arms around his old comrade. It was a momentous moment for both. It still might not be "too late"—those fatal, fatal words which had so often provided the epitaph for the unprepared. There might still be time left to build a decent defense here in these lovely Islands against sudden Japanese aggression.

"All that we have, all that we are, is yours," the dramatic, impulsive President of the Commonwealth uttered. It was a re-birth of hope that filled his heart.

Theirs was to be an eternal comradeship in arms. They might have something to fight with now. Weapons, tanks, planes, guns, ammunition and money certainly would now start flowing across the Pacific to them. It would help, even if it were only a trickle compared to the flood of supplies pouring across the Atlantic to Britain and Russia.

MacArthur, too, was like a man suddenly reprieved from a death sentence. He had a chance now—even though it were only a slim one. Time was of the essence; time to arm and prepare.

There was not a second to be lost. Along with the announce-ment of the landing of Japanese troops in Indo-China, the papers that Sunday morning carried the story that Japan had called up a million reservists. Already she had 600,000 troops in Man-churia, and certainly more than that number in China. On the great island bastion of Formosa—a bare seven hundred miles north of Manila—there were many divisions of highly trained, experienced invasion troops, and innumerable airplanes. The Japanese Navy was on a full war footing; for almost four years it had been fighting against China.

Every Chinese port and harbor of consequence, except British

Hong Kong, was in the hands of the Japanese. Everywhere there were Japanese naval, ground and air concentrations. Moderate men had made their last stand in Japan. Exactly eight days before this momentous Sunday morning, a new cabinet had been formed under Prince Konoye—but he had been forced to retain the war-minded Tojo as Minister of War. It was Tojo who had led the movement against democratic methods in the Island Kingdom. Japan was at last on the loose in the Western Pacific, and it was only a question of When, Where, and How the certain attack against the Philippines would come.

Quietly MacArthur read again the two telegrams, and then began to formulate the successive steps necessary to comply with his orders. The first thing was to plan the details of mobilization of the Philippine native army at the earliest possible moment that camps could be built and an organization set up. He had had neither the money nor the authorization to do this before. Next, requisitions for arms and supplies would have to be made, and the shipments started from the States. He would let the regular Department of the Philippines, that controlled the American Army and the Philippine Scouts, and was now under Major General Grunert, continue for the time being to function under its present organization as an echelon of the main command. A separate General Headquarters for these brand new United States Army Forces in the Far East—to be called USAFFE—would have to be set up immediately and start working on the hundred and one details of mobilization.

That was Number One on the list, the mobilization of the hundred and fifty thousand sturdy half-trained rice farmers and city clerks and school boys as fast as camps could be built. Then they would have to be whipped into regiments, and finally into fighting divisions. Time was what he needed now—six, seven, eight months of precious time—to do at this late date the things that he had asked more than once for the chance to do.

At three that Sunday afternoon Sutherland and Marshall were to report back with as many details of the mobilization as they could work out in that short time. Always now that word "time" would be the ruling factor. Time would soon bring D-day.

D-day was when Japan would strike.

* * * *

For almost six years there had been two distinct military organizations, and each had been more or less charged with the task of defending the 1,400 far-scattered Philippine Islands. The senior force was the U. S. Army, which included the able and experienced Philippine Scouts; this was the Department of the Philippines, U. S. Army. The second defense force was the Philippine Army, with an alert Philippine soldier, Major General Basil Valdes, as Chief of Staff; actually this Philippine Army had been planned, organized and developed by MacArthur and a small group of U. S. Army officers loaned by the American government to the Commonwealth of the Philippines.

On this historic day in July, 1941, the forces under the Department of the Philippines, Major General Grunert commanding, consisted of 12,000 Philippine Scouts and about half that number of American soldiers. Except for the gallant, old 31st Infantry, and the very tiny Air Force, the bulk of the remaining Americans were Coast Artillerymen planted on Corregidor, and the supporting defenses at the entrance to Manila Bay. For a full year Grunert had been pounding away at the War Department for more men, equipment, reserve ammunition and war preparation. On January 25th he received authority to bring the Scouts up to their maximum authorized strength of 12,000 men. Enlistment over the Islands was started immediately, and, with the full approval of General MacArthur, only Filipinos who had received the initial five and a half months' intensive training of the Filipino Army reservists were accepted. Within a month the quota was filled. By the end of March, 1941, there had been brought up to strength the 45th and 57th Infantry Regiments, the 26th Cavalry, and the 24th Field Artillery and certain specialist units, all belonging to the Philippine Scouts. Including the American troops, the actual forces under the Department of the Philippines was a grand total of 18,000 on this morning when MacArthur took over.

The picture of the Philippine Army was an entirely different one. The overall defense scheme that MacArthur had worked out in 1935, contemplated that when full Independence came in 1946 the Philippine Commonwealth would have a force of between 400,000 and 500,000 trained and equipped men. Each year in the ten-year period 40,000 new trainees were to be given five and a half months' intensive initial training, with refresher courses each succeeding year. In local armories would be the uniform and equipment for each man. Upon mobilization orders he would report to his armory, get his outfit, and repair immediately to a given point where he would join his unit. The advancement from platoon and company units up to full army divisions was to progress systematically, and at the end of ten years the complete defense would emerge as a coordinated, effective military entity primarily based on thirty infantry divisions. To facilitate all this the Islands had been divided into ten Military Districts, and in each there would finally be three Infantry Divisions, and special units.

Besides these ground forces there would ultimately be an Off Shore Patrol of between 100 and 200 swift PT mosquito boats; and an Air Force of between 1,000 and 1,500 first-line planes.

In the early days of the plans the War Department had materially helped out by the loan of discarded World War Enfield rifles and Lewis and Browning machine guns, and the allocation of certain batteries of old 75 mm. guns for artillery training. The U. S. Navy was skeptical at this time of the usefulness of PT boats, so MacArthur, and his competent Naval adviser, Lt. Commander Sidney Huff, U. S. Navy retired, were forced to purchase their initial pair of mosquito boats in England. The additional boats were actually to be built in the Islands and the engines purchased abroad. The first pilot model had been completed and two boats had already arrived from England. . . . The Air Force program was likewise held back by the lack of equipment; a few post-dated training planes, however, had been loaned by the U. S. Army Air Corps, and a beginning made in what promised to be a splendid and efficient native air arm.

In the scant six years that MacArthur had been working on these sound and adequate defense ideas, he had disheartening discouragements and rebuffs. Often Washington itself had found reasons to disparage the whole plan of an adequate defense of this vulnerable advance Pacific base of ours. It was clear that either we must hold the Philippine outpost or get out of the Western Pacific entirely. With the advent of the long-range airplane it was doubly imperative that if we remained we must have secure airfields and naval bases in these islands. We could not have our cake and eat it too. We either must build and defend our bases in this Far Eastern World, or we must abandon them.

MacArthur was accustomed to bitter opposition. He had constantly stood for advancement in defense preparations, and believed that "Wars are won in the future not in the past." He had consistently and incessantly fought those who stood against his country's good, and those who had opposed its being adequately defended. The dignity and assurance of the man conveyed a sense of victory and success—yet his battles were bitter ones against powerful opponents and he did not always win.

His life had been dedicated to the service of his country. Early in his military career he had learned the folly of unpreparedness, and he had fought against it with every skill and determination he could muster. Returning from distinguished service with the Rainbow Division in the World War, he had been appointed Superintendent of the United States Military Academy at West Point. It was one of the most important assignments in the peacetime army.

A half hundred senior Generals were embittered at this assignment but Secretary of War Newton D. Baker felt that the Military Academy must be completely modernized and reinspired. MacArthur, then just turned thirty-nine, was chosen for this delicate job. Despite bitter opposition from both within and without, his success was complete and he modeled a new West Point in the spirit of old West Point. He completely reoriented the direction of military training and thought, bringing it fully abreast of the time. "To be clean, to live clean and to think clean" was his constant preachment. Probably no Superintendent since the Academy's great founder, Major Sylvanus Thayer, has left so indelible a mark on this great military college. The fruits of his success are being reaped today on every battlefield in the world.

From West Point he was sent to the Philippines as commander of the newly created Post of Manila; then assigned to command the Infantry Brigade at Fort McKinley, and later promoted to a Major General and given the command of the Philippine Division. It was during this period that the United States Congress passed the dangerous 1924 Exclusion Act. Japan was bitter and aroused. Her militarists hid their anger and bided their time. Their revenge would come. The danger was growing.

Back in the United States MacArthur in 1925 was given a Corps Area command and three years later returned to the Philippine Islands as Department Commander in supreme military command. There he saw once again how pitifully inadequate our defenses were. His visits to Japan, and the intelligence reports he was receiving, proved all too clearly how dangerous the situation was becoming. He knew his Japan. He had been Aide to his father, during the latter part of the time when the senior MacArthur was Chief Military Observer with the Japanese Army in the war against Russia. He had met many of the famous Japanese commanders. Among them was Admiral Togo, the hero of the swift, treacherous attack on the Russian fleet at Port Arthur in the spring of 1904—an act that was to be repeated in all its brutal cunning at Pearl Harbor thirty-seven years later.

Back in Washington as Chief of Staff from 1930 to 1935, MacArthur threw himself into the great task of first saving and then modernizing the U. S. skeleton army. It was just that—a skeleton army, starved to death by a disinterested Congress, an ignorant public, and a nation-wide inertia and indifference, that guaranteed from the start that his crusade would be a lost cause. It was for his country and not for himself that he fought. The personal insults, checks and defeats he suffered were impersonal to him; it was his country that must pay the price for his failure to awaken stubborn people to the dangers ahead.

His prophetic reports of what was coming, his warnings of the total inadequacy of our military establishment, found impatient listeners. Yet, in spite of all, by his tireless insistence he saved the nucleus and laid the foundations for the modern army which fights today. His views on war are still the guiding star of our best military thought.

In 1935 he came to Manila with his brilliant dream of building here in the friendly Philippines a force of a half-million men who not only could hold the Islands against aggression, but could form the first line, the outer defenses, of America herself. Before two years were up opposition developed at home and abroad that threatened to wreck the entire plan. He was accused of forcing a great conscription army on the poor Islands; of building an imperial, dictatorial role for himself, and for Quezon. He was interfering with the white imperialists in the Philippines and in the whole East. And who was certain, anyway, that the Filipinos would really fight?

So far-reaching was this pressure that toward the end of 1937 the schemers planned to force him home, and thus let the whole great dream of an adequate Philippine defense bog down under its own helpless weight. He was ordered home to report for duty. Quezon pleaded with him to remain on as Military Adviser, and see the plan through. Quezon would have agreed to no other officer as a substitute.

MacArthur respectfully asked his President to permit him to retire; he had been in the Army for more than thirty-eight years; he had been a General Officer for nineteen years. In order to stay on here and finish his job, he was being forced to retire. A letter of regretful approval came from the President—and on December 31, 1937, Douglas MacArthur's name was taken off the Active List of the United States Army. Once again he had been personally thwarted and humiliated. Once again frustration was to be his reward. But he kept on. His vision told him his country some day would need a loyal Philippine Army. That was all that was important to him.

He said nothing but smiled his grim and infrequent smile. Then this determined soldier turned to his job of building up the Philippine defense, of making strong this outer bastion of his country's security. The going was not easy. His own countrymen, in Manila and outside, hammered away at him. Certain native politicians, concerned by the military appropriations, small as they were, found reasons to oppose him. The cost of running the Constabulary was finally saddled on him; and by the time his 1941 training budget was made his army appropriations, entirely inadequate at best, had been reduced by half. Yet the war clouds were now sweeping down the China Sea, and it was obvious that nothing in the world but a complete acceptance of Japanese domination of this part of the world could keep war from coming.

In Washington the nation's leaders had shifted the eyes and might of America towards the European scene. A wide ocean separated America from the actual contest and the danger. Yet for the Philippines, where American men and land and honor were directly under the threat of a treacherous attack by a bitter, fanatical and determined Japan, little was done. Even the Pacific fleet was divided and part sent to the Atlantic. This act was the electric signal to Tokyo. *Der Tag* was now possible.

MacArthur and his worried Staff could only stand by and hope —and futilely press their claims for help. Early in the spring of 1941 the General offered his services to President Roosevelt. Then on this Sunday morning in late July came the sudden orders for the formation of this brand new USAFFE—United States Army Forces Far East—with himself in command. It might still not be too late to meet the Japanese attack.

His long-range plan for the Philippine native army had not quite reached the stage where the small training units of platoons, companies and batteries had been incorporated into regiments and divisions. There had been neither the time nor the money to bring these small units into suitable camps where large organizational training could be carried out.

Within twenty-four hours of the arrival of the orders from Washington, a hurriedly collected USAFFE staff was put to work on this problem of mobilization and training. And twenty-four hours after that, previous plans were well enough implemented to be able to set September 1st as the day when the mobilization would actually start. That left roughly thirty days to pick camp sites, build roads, water tanks, nipa huts, and buildings where the thousands of reservists could be brought together for regimental training.

Other staff officers were working night and day on the requisitions for equipment, guns, ammunition, planes and the hundred and one critical items for an army in being. All had to be perfectly synchronized; the speed of the mobilization had to mesh into the progress of camp construction; this, in turn, had to fit into the securing of equipment and heavy weapons.

Across MacArthur's desk came conflicting demands and needs. Adequate air protection had been one of the fundamental ideas of the old long-range plan. A series of open and secret air fields were to be built that would stretch from southern Mindanao up the thousand miles to the very northern tip of Luzon. The most important fields were to be concentrated in the islands of the Inner Sea—"Mare Nostrum," MacArthur used to term this key middle part of the Philippine Archipelago. He had conceived the idea of mounting coast defense guns at the several entrances to this Inland Sea. Once this was done, and proper airfields constructed and equipped, an Air Force installed, PT boats secured, and their bases and supplies built and guarded, the vital problem of feeding MacArthur's armies would be solved. Small supply boats with food could move from these rich granaries of the south, from Cebu, from Negros and Samar, from Panay and Bohol, and work their way safely up through a protected inner sea to the great northern island of Luzon and its key Manila Bay.

The adequate defense of this Inland Sea was one of the vital parts of the whole over-all defense plan. But it took proper equipment, big guns, trained forces, supplies, planes, boats—and plenty of money—to put it into being. All these were automatically shut off from MacArthur when the great decision was made in Washington to throw the full weight of America into the European war. During that critical six months' period before July, 1941, when America was being drawn willy-nilly into the frightful European maelstrom, the Philippines and their defenses received scant attention. Almost all that was actually done was to authorize in the early months of 1941, that the Philippine Scouts be doubled in size. Yet war with Japan was moving down with almost the speed of the winds.

Stored safely in grease in American arsenals prior to this time were a number of World War 155's—six-inch guns. There were also certain eight-inch rifles, actually of the vintage of 1898, that had been taken off railroad-artillery flat cars and put on disappearing mounts. Exactly twenty-four of these 155's and seven eight-inch rifles, had been dispatched to Manila, ultimately to be installed to block the channels of MacArthur's Inland Sea. But no money went with the guns, and $2,000,000 was the minimum sum that would be required. It was a blessing, however, that on the day USAFFE was formed these weapons were on hand.

Bill Marquat, coast artillery expert in the new USAFFE Staff, at once picked Major Guy H. Stubbs and Captain Steve Mellnik of the Coast Artillery Corps stationed on Corregidor, and turned over to them the task of mounting these guns into key positions around the Inland Sea in the quickest possible time. (It was this same Steve Mellnik, by the way, who two years later helped lead the initial group to escape from the Jap prison camps in Mindanao, and gave to the world the first authentic story of the horrible treatment meted out to our prisoners of war in the Islands. Major Stubbs was too weak to attempt the trek that led to liberty.)

Always the real enemy now was Time. Would there be precious time enough to mobilize the Philippine Army, train it, equip it and weld it into a fighting force? Would there be time for the guns of the Inland Sea to be installed, for the series of airfields to be built, and would the new planes and their pilots arrive in time from the States? Would sufficient arms

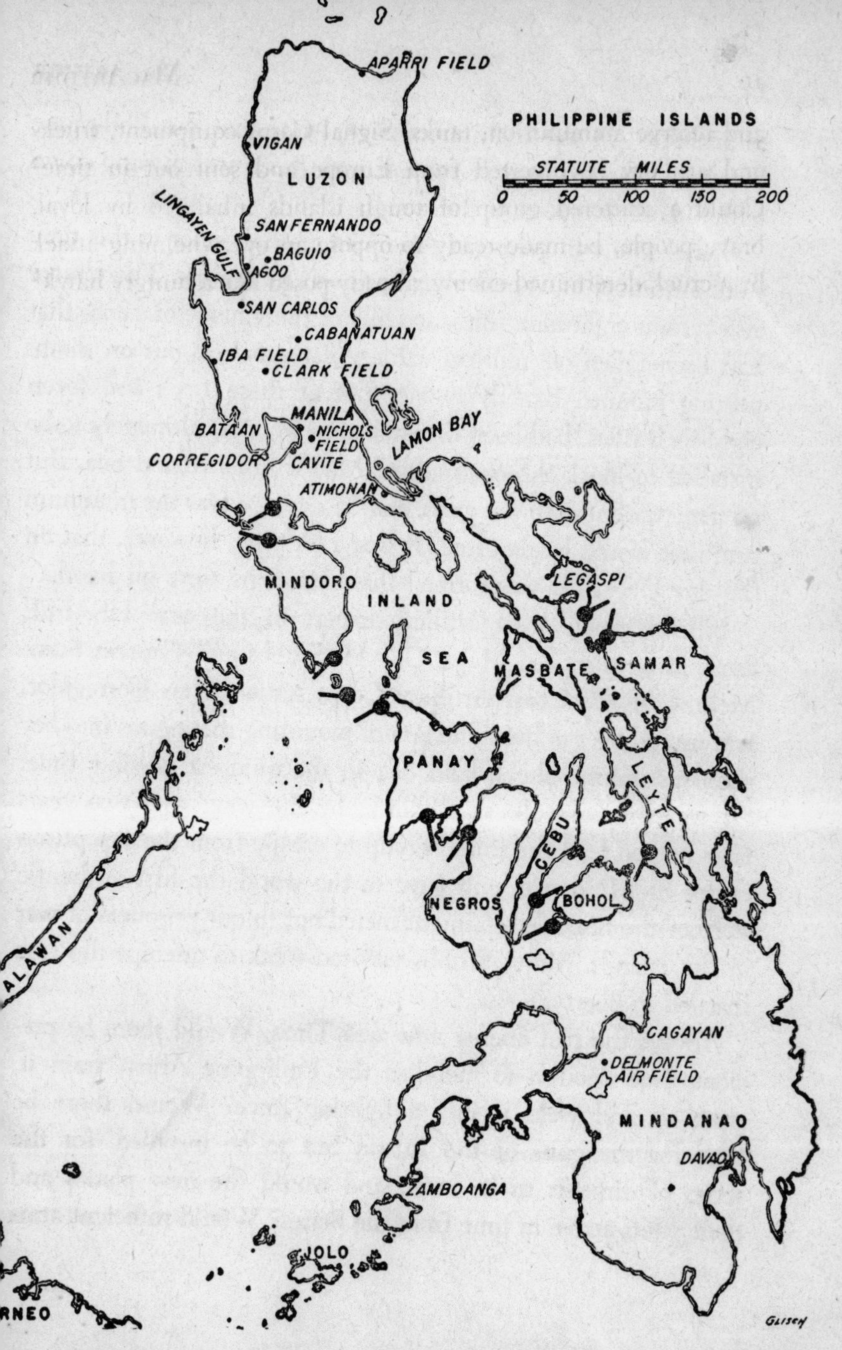

How MacArthur planned to set heavy coastal guns at the entrances to the and Sea, and build here in the heart of the Philippines, a great, self-contained tress.

and reserve ammunition, tanks, Signal Corps equipment, trucks and artillery be diverted from Europe and sent out in time? Could a scattered group of tough islands inhabited by loyal, brave people, be made ready to oppose an overwhelming attack by a cruel, determined enemy, already posed like a hungry hawk?

CHAPTER TWO

LONG AGO THE MANY PROBLEMS OF WAR WITH THE JAPANESE had been thought out by MacArthur. They were part of his great coordinated over-all plan of defense. Yet it had been made useless by the complete indifference of the highest authorities.

But no moment now was spent in vain regret that so little had been done; rather there was a splendid optimism that now something might be done that would count. If we were not thrust into war before the end of March, 1942—and if proper help would be sent in the meantime from the States—the Philippines could be made into a hard, if not an impossible, nut for Japan to crack. It would at least take her full military, naval and air might to break down these islands—if time were kind.

Precious days galloped by. Crisis followed crisis. Four days after USAFFE was formed, Japan demanded bases in Thailand, and full control over the tin and rubber and rice plantations there. And Secretary of Navy Knox announced that Japan had on hand from fourteen to sixteen months' oil reserve. A week later, Tokyo openly warned she would resist encirclement by the democracies; and Darlan became Chief of the Vichy puppet government.

On Luzon a thousand and more native carpenters were working day and night erecting army camps, and the first mobilization units were being designated, when on August 15th, the papers carried the startling news that Roosevelt and Churchill had met at sea, and promulgated the Atlantic Charter. Five days later Japan announced the forced detention of one hundred American citizens. It came as a strange answer to the Atlantic world. On August 17th the tiny but eager Philippine Army Air Force was formally inducted into the United States Army. Faster was the pace; closer came the rising danger.

September 1st was a red letter day. The transport *Meigs* arrived with a cargo of army trucks, and certain other critical equipment. This first of September would be a memorable one for another reason too; this day the first ten regiments of the Philippine native army were inducted into the U. S. service. Those busy carpenters had thrown together sufficient camp facilities to take care of a single regiment in each of the ten Military Districts. Five of these were in the main island of Luzon, and the rest scattered about the other islands. Besides the single regiment of infantry mobilized in each district, all Filipino commissioned officers and all non-commissioned officers of the rank of sergeant, and certain specialists, were called up for special training.

Things were really moving now. Time and equipment and supplies were all that were needed. MacArthur had the know-how. One U. S. Lt. Colonel and three additional regular officers were sent to each divisional area; and two Regular Army officers went to each battalion; and one non-commissioned officer and two or three specialists to each company.

Methodically, yet with every possible acceleration, this army of mountain boys, carabao drivers and lads from the streets, was coming into being. Every day of grace was a godsend. It was a race against war. On September 10th, Nazi U-boats sank two U. S. cargo ships carrying contraband supplies to belligerents; and a day or two later Roosevelt announced that U. S. vessels would fire on any ship molesting our right to neutral trade.

September 26th was another big day for MacArthur. That day

the U.S.S. *President Coolidge* tied up to the dock in Manila, and while eager bystanders cheered, American troops began rolling down the gangplanks; the 200th Coast Artillery Anti-Aircraft Regiment; the 194th Tank Battalion; two full ordnance companies; and a ship's belly full of ammunition and supplies.

Four days later Japan reaffirmed her pact with the Axis powers. And two days after that Vice Air Marshal Brooke-Popham, Commander-in-Chief of Singapore and British Malaya, arrived in Manila for a visit. Almost simultaneously the good old 4th Marines arrived from the death trap of Shanghai. They would be available for Bataan and Corregidor.

A week later Tojo kicked out the Konoye Cabinet and installed himself as Premier and War Minister. There was no single check on the mad militarists now; they had the only pass to the Emperor's presence. Their will was his will. It spelled out WAR, unless Washington was willing to stall along until defenses in the Islands could be built.

On October 10th the Philippine Scouts, with Manila's old pride and joy, the Thirty-first Infantry, were made into the First Philippine Division. A tough, lean cavalryman, Brig. General Jonathan Wainwright, a protege of MacArthur when they were Cadets at West Point, was given command. MacArthur was now spending considerable of his time visiting camps and training centers, inspiring the native units, personally inducting them into U. S. service, and in a score of ways making his calm confidence and fighting spirit a model for this little army. There was still so little with which to do so much. His native soldiers had only their old pre-World War Enfield rifles, an inadequate number of machine guns, and trench mortars that were twenty-five years old. They had scanty uniforms and instead of steel hats they wore pith helmets that shone like silver in the warm sunlight. But they had spirit—and they looked to MacArthur as their true leader and their hero. They were an army without shoes, but they had bright banners—and a cause.

That day when the Scouts became the First Philippine Division, MacArthur turned to Wainwright and said: "Jonathan, I'm forming a North Luzon Force and a South Luzon Force. Which do you want?"

Wainwright chose the North Force. He would lead it well and bravely. He would make history with it. He had followed his Chief at West Point as first Captain of the Corps, he would follow him again into the bloody welter of battle with the same old faith and confidence.

October was sweeping across the red-tinted skies. On the 13th the Dutch Chief of Staff, Hain ter Poorten, arrived in Manila. November 4th, Major General Brereton alighted from the China Clipper and took over the Air Force. Planes had been dribbling in—one for every fifty sent across the Atlantic. That next day Rear Admiral Rockwell reported. Then Armistice Day broke.

It was a day not to be forgotten soon, for ten thousand miles away in Washington three men were to sit down to play a deadly game. One was Judge Hull, Secretary of State; the other two were the Japanese Ambassador, Admiral Nomura, and the grinning Special Envoy Kurusu. Both MacArthur and Quezon knew Kurusu well; for years he had been Consul General in Manila.

Surely the days of grace were numbered now. Those ominous war clouds were quickly becoming blacker and blacker. Time was running out, for there seemed little chance that Japan would accept the American demand that she renounce her ambitions. She had committed herself to conquest, and there could be no pulling back.

On November 15th Philippine Commonwealth Day was celebrated. There were short addresses—but tears were behind the shining eyes of Quezon as he spoke so bravely. The bugles sounded Retreat, and while the military band played the National Anthems the flags of the United States and of the Commonwealth were slowly lowered together. No one there would ever forget the sight.

On November 24th eight more native infantry regiments and six new Field Artillery regiments were inducted into the U. S. Service. Guns had been arriving, and for more than two months Philippine artillery units had been under intensive training at Fort O'Donnell near Stotsenberg, sixty-five miles north of Manila.

Terrible and deadly things were happening almost every day now. On November 27th in Washington, Hull handed the two Japanese emissaries a final ultimatum. Three days later Litvinoff arrived from Singapore on his way to Washington. That was Thanksgiving Day. There was real rejoicing in Manila, for on that day the transports *Coolidge* and *Scott* arrived with reinforcements and a batch of much-needed officers.

Messages of grave warning were arriving constantly from Washington. Early in November MacArthur had placed Corregidor defenses on a full alert. The anti-aircraft guns and the batteries were manned twenty-four hours a day. All leaves were cancelled and every final preparation was made. All bus lines and civilian transport in Luzon had been requisitioned and troops moved. Regiments had been brought together in Divisional organizations. For months the Staffs had been trained and indoctrinated.

Quietly MacArthur made his final dispositions of such forces as he had. In Wainwright's North Luzon Force there were three native midget divisions—the 11th, 21st and 31st, with half the 71st that would be brought in from the central islands. Besides these native troops there was the experienced First Philippine Division, made up of Scouts and American troops—and the 26th Cavalry belonging to the Scouts.

The South Luzon Force consisted of the 41st and 51st Philippine Divisions and a special division made up of Constabulary Troops. There was also one-half the 91st Division, which, like the half of the 71st, would be ferried up from the Southern Islands. Each of these native divisions numbered only around eight thousand men, and they were in reality little more than the three infantry regiments of the normal Triangular Division. One regiment in each division had had three full months of regimental training; a second regiment one and one-half months; while the third regiment was mobilized at the very last moment, with no regimental training at all. To each of these small divisions was assigned some artillery, but all the special troops such as Signal Corps, Engineers, and Transport, belonged to a general GHQ pool, and were assigned to the various outfits as the need arose.

The total forces MacArthur had to hold this key island of Luzon were a little more than 60,000 natives of the Philippine Army, most of whom were infantrymen; 12,000 Philippine Scouts, who had long been an integral part of the regular United States Army; and 18,000 American white forces, including the Air Corps, two tank battalions and the garrisons on Corregidor and the island forts. Added together this gives a grand total of 30,000 American and Philippine Regulars, and 60,000 native troops of the Philippine National Army. For the most part they were armed with antiquated First World War weapons, and completely lacked the special units and equipment that made up modern regimental teams, well-balanced divisions and efficient corps. It was a hastily thrown together, partially trained, half-equipped army of patriots, who fought for a cause and a beloved leader.

MacArthur's grand plan was to gain time for reinforcements to come from the United States. The Navy was charged with keeping the way open. Meanwhile he hoped to hold on until adequate help came.

He expected that the most important Japanese landings would be made at several beaches in Lingayen Gulf on the China Sea, roughly 120 miles northwestward from Manila. Doubtless other feints and smaller landings would be made in North Luzon, while there would be at least one large attempt to land south of Manila.

Manila was the hub from which radiated the spokes of the North and South Forces. It was protected from the sea by the great rock fortress of Corregidor, thirty miles across the Bay. This fortress was antiquated and vulnerable. Before the advent of air power, it was powerful enough to withstand any sea attack. Against air it was little more than a hollow shell with its exposed installations and its open and limited water and power plants. MacArthur's strategy was to keep Manila Bay open for the Navy already there and for the Naval relief that would come. He would gather together his troops and supplies on Bataan Peninsula, that swung like a protecting arm toward the entrance to Manila Bay. On this ultimate side-slip retirement into the Peninsula would depend the fate of his army and of Corregidor itself. For this Peninsula of Bataan, rising from the sea only three miles to the north of Corregidor Fortress, was the key to the Rock that locked the entrance to the bay. Once Bataan fell, the enemy could put his heavy guns on the slopes of Mariveles Mountain, and shell Corregidor into starvation and submission. It was Corregidor that was the most exposed and vulnerable target, not Bataan.

Work had been pushed with utmost speed on a number of new airfields over the Islands, but most of them were only half-completed when December crowded out hectic November. In north-central Mindanao, 500 miles south of Manila, there was a single great bomber field base called Del Monte field; on the outskirts of Manila was Nichols Field for fighters; and sixty-five miles to the north was Clark Field, still crude and primitive by modern standards. There were minor air strips that could be pressed into emergency use near the beaches at Aparri and Vigan in Northern Luzon, and at Legaspi in Southern Luzon.

Early in December a squadron of eighteen P-40's was quickly unloaded and assembled in Manila. They had yet to be "slow timed"—which means having their engines slowly broken in—and their guns bored, sighted and tested. Including this squadron, Major General Brereton could muster exactly seventy-two first-line pursuit planes for immediate service, and exactly thirty-five Flying Fortresses. These Fortresses had been ordered south to the safety of Mindanao. He had besides a few antiquated pursuits, and a handful of obsolete bombers.

The Asiatic Fleet, under the command of aging Admiral Hart, consisted of two cruisers, eighteen old four-stacker destroyers, twenty-seven submarines, mostly pre-World War design, and six PT boats. The tiny Philippine fleet, bought and paid for out of Philippine funds, consisted of Huff's two PT boats made in England, and a third one that had been launched on August 5th.

Besides these armed forces of the ground, sea and air, there was the fine skill, the stout heart and the indomitable will of Douglas MacArthur. He was even at this date the idol of the Philippine soldiery. The MacArthurs, father and son, had been a living part of the Filipinos' long fight for independence and full liberty. Lieutenant General Arthur MacArthur had planned, with Brig. General Fred Funston, the coup that had resulted in the capture of the Philippine revolutionary leader General Aguinaldo. The elder MacArthur had treated the captured Filipino chieftain as a full brother in arms, and this one gesture had had much to do with bringing about in 1900 the voluntary proclamation by Aguinaldo that brought the insurrection to a close.

It was this same Arthur MacArthur who, as Military Governor of Manila in 1900, laid down the basic judicial code of justice and equality, based primarily on the right of habeas corpus, which had established individual freedom and liberty for the Filipinos. He had laid the foundations for both the Philippine Constabulary and the Philippine Scouts, and originated the basic thought that the Filipinos should be prepared ultimately to defend their own country. He had opened the door of a new world to these gentle, kindly people. His son, Douglas MacArthur, was to keep it open.

By some mysterious, instinctive way all this was known deep in the hearts of the plain people of these Philippine Islands. Douglas MacArthur had spent in all fourteen years among these people. He had become almost a part of them. He had fought for their rights; he had believed in their independence. He had never once exploited them for national gain. He had taught them to be soldiers against the day when their liberties, their soil and their honor would be assailed. That day was now at hand.

On December 3rd, 4th and 5th, foreign planes were reported over the northern and central portions of Luzon at daybreak, flying high. MacArthur ordered that our fighters drive them off or shoot them down if they invaded again.

Daily messages from Washington told of the almost certain failure of the Japanese negotiations. War apparently could not be avoided, unless either Japan or the United States made a complete about-face.

Here in Manila, ten thousand miles to the westward, there was intense anxiety. Beginning as far back as November 15th all pursuit aircraft had been kept fully gassed, armed and on constant alert twenty-four hours a day. Pilots were available on thirty minutes' call, and on December 6th Major General Brereton held a conference and placed all units on alert, with combat crews, enlisted men and officers constantly ready for duty.

An aircraft warning system had been built up with native air watchers who relayed their reports by telephone to the Interceptor Headquarters at Nielson Field near Manila; from here they were relayed by teletype to the plotting board at Clark Field, sixty miles north. One radar set was functioning at Iba, on the China Sea coast in Zambales Province; a second set was in the process of being installed; and a third set actually en route to Legaspi.

Colonel Spencer Akin of the U. S. Army Signal Corps had taken over the entire telephone system of the Island. Under the general direction of the able and energetic Joe Stevenot, head of the Telephone Company, a competent communication network was set up and ready. Every telephone switchboard girl in the

Island was an eager, loyal watcher. Their acts of pure heroism in the days to come were to become legendary.

By the night of December 7th General MacArthur had made his final dispositions to meet a surprise attack at any moment. He was certain that when it came it would come without formal declaration of war. His memory was still vivid of Port Arthur and a treacherous gray dawn in March, 1904.

He and his men were as ready as Time and outside neglect and indifference would let them be. There was nothing to do now but wait.

At 4:30 on the Monday morning of December 8th Philippine time—which was Sunday in the U. S.—the phone rang in the Chief of Staff's office at GHQ in 1 Victoria Street, Manila. Dick Sutherland, grabbing a bit of sleep on a cot, picked up the receiver. "The Japs have attacked Pearl Harbor," was the startling news.

He ordered that all commanders be notified that a state of war existed. Then he reached for the phone that was on the secret direct line to General MacArthur's bedroom in the Manila Hotel. The General answered personally, and Sutherland gave him the tragic message.

"Pearl Harbor!" he repeated incredulously. "It should be our strongest point." Then he added, "Thanks, Dick," and hung up the receiver.

There was little he could do for the next few hours. Every contingency, every possibility, had been thought out and met to the best of the means at hand.

Well, he'd fight them on the beaches, and on the mountain trails and down the valley roads. He'd fight them to the last man and the last cartridge and last ounce of food. He had never been beaten in his five campaigns of the World War. Perhaps this would be different.

Quietly he reached for his Bible where he had laid it down beside his bed that night.

CHAPTER THREE

AT 3:30 MONDAY MORNING, DECEMBER 8TH—ALMOST AN HOUR before any word reached Manila—the commercial radio station at Clark Field picked up a message that Pearl Harbor was being bombed.

It had come out of the blue—without confirmation or genesis. The air had been full of wild rumors and reports these days; this might be just another canard. But this operator took no chances. He notified Headquarters at the field, and in turn the Base Commander was given the report. All units on the field were double alerted, and Clark Field's 3rd and 20th Pursuit squadrons were ordered to stand by. These squadrons were normally of eighteen planes each, but the usual thirty to forty percent were grounded for repairs and overhauls.

At four o'clock that morning the radar at Iba, on the China Sea coast, reported an unidentified air formation approximately seventy-five miles off the coast heading towards Corregidor. The 3rd Squadron of P-40 E's was dispatched to intercept. But it was still dark, and due to lack of full altitude data from the radar, no contact was made. The excited men on the plotting board traced the approaching aircraft as they swung off to the west, and out of range of the pursuit.

At 4:45 that morning official news came from Manila to Clark Field that a state of war existed. At 9:30 a large force of enemy bombers was reported over Lingayen heading towards Manila, some 120 miles to the southeastward. The 17th Squadron of pursuit took off from Nichols Field, outside Manila, with the mission of covering Clark Field. At the same moment the 20th Squadron left Clark Field to intercept the reported enemy over nearby Rosales—but no contact was made. When it had reached a point approximately thirty miles from Rosales, this enemy force turned to the northeast, bombed Baguio—then disappeared to the north.

When the 20th Squadron of Pursuits had taken off from Clark Field at 9:30 the Base Commander there immediately ordered the seventeen Flying Fortresses into the air. They were fully gassed and bomb loaded. One of the forts had earlier in the morning started on a reconnaissance flight over Formosa, but when it ran into overcast skies it returned home. All that morning the crews of these Forts had stood by ready for instant flight.

Besides these seventeen Fortresses at Clark Field, there were eighteen others five hundred miles to the south at Del Monte Field on Mindanao. Several days before this fatal morning of December 8th, while all the Fortresses were still at Clark Field, MacArthur, through his Chief of Staff, Sutherland, had ordered all four squadrons to Mindanao, where they would be safe from a sneak attack.

It was deadly clear in MacArthur's mind that these ships would be in constant danger while on the ground at Clark Field. Normal dispersal formation gave normal protection against high, horizontal bombing, but as long as the big planes were on the ground they could be knocked off by dive bombers as easy as you should shoot fish in a barrel. The only safe course was to base the Fortresses far to the south at Mindanao, out of range of any possible land-based enemy planes.

The approved mission of these big bombers was to sink approaching enemy fleets and convoys. With their all-out range of two thousand miles they could fly, under battle condition, between seven and eight hundred miles to a mission and then return under their own power. This meant that they could cover from the safe base in Del Monte, Mindanao, the threatened waters around Lingayen Bay and the beach-heads on the lower peninsula of Luzon, and still have enough gas left to return to their home field. Or they could be flown first to Clark Field, where they could be gassed and loaded with bombs—and then sent on their mission. They could fly back to the safety of Mindanao once their mission was completed. (Turn back to map on page 15.)

Compliance with MacArthur's initial order, sent through the channel of his Chief of Staff, was delayed. He was told that the bombers were not quite ready to make the trip. A second time Sutherland ordered the bombers south. Again there was a delay, and the bombers did not take off.

A third time—and only a day or two before tragedy came—MacArthur, through Sutherland, again ordered the Fortresses to be sent south to safety. This time the order was peremptory and final. Eighteen of the thirty-five were moved. For some unannounced and still unknown reason the remaining seventeen delayed at Clark Field.

And now a little after 9:30 on this morning of December 8th these seventeen Fortresses still at Clark Field, north of Manila, took to the air. The 20th Pursuit Squadron had just taken off, and the bombers followed them immediately. If the enemy was heading for Clark Field certainly those Fortresses would want to be off the ground and high in the air.

The large enemy flight that had suddenly swung off from its course to bomb Baguio, and then had flown north, was no longer a problem. The All Clear was sounded and the Forts were ordered back to the field. The 20th Pursuit Squadron covered the landing, and then returned to the field itself for regassing. The Fortresses, of course, could have kept to the sky for a full ten hours. Why the local commander ordered them brought down from the safety of the limitless skies to the constant danger of attack on the ground at Clark Field still remains a mystery.

It was now 11:30. Here on Clark Field were the seventeen Fortresses, and the 20th and 17th Pursuit Squadrons. A message announced that a large formation of enemy bombers was reported over the China Sea approaching Manila. The 3rd Pursuit Squadron was dispatched from Nichols Field, Manila, to intercept, and the 17th Pursuit was sent up from Clark Field to cover the sky over Bataan. The 34th Pursuit Squadron at Nichols Field, was placed on standing patrol over Manila.

At 11:45 a report was received of an enemy formation over Lingayen Gulf, some sixty or seventy miles to the northwest of Clark Field. The formation was moving south. The 21st Pursuit Squadron at Del Carmen was ordered to cover Clark Field. This 21st Squadron, however, was flying old P-35's that were little more than death crates. Fearlessly they went out to meet the cream of the Japanese air force.

On the ground at Clark Field the ships of the 20th Pursuit were being gassed, while the fighter pilots were grabbing a bite of lunch. It was a slow job gassing the bright ships, because of inadequate facilities. Again it was a case of too little and too late.

On the dispersal areas and "hard standings" sat the seventeen Fortresses. Most of them were dispersed, but there was one flight of four lined up in a row. Ordinary caution would have had them in the air; if MacArthur's orders had been carried out they would have been operating from the safe base in Del Monte Field, five hundred miles to the south. But his orders were not carried out.

At 12:15 the last ship of the 20th Pursuit Squadron had finished its gassing, and the squadron was ordered to take off and cover the field. Four of the P-40's had just taken to the air, when fifty-four enemy bombers and an undetermined number of dive bombers struck the field. The four pursuits were knocked down, and five on the take-off and five on the ground were destroyed by strafing. All the seventeen Fortresses were bombed and machine gunned, and only two were ever to fly again.

A direct hit on the communications center destroyed ground-to-air control of fighters in the air. The field was now doubly helpless.

The tragic news of the disaster was telephoned to Headquarters in Manila. General MacArthur was informed at once.

He was grave but utterly calm. There was no time for regret or recrimination. It was the fortunes of war; and this experienced commander knew that most of the breaks would continue to be against him. At best he could only hold on until help of some kind or other would come to him. He was not concerned at this moment of danger with the reason for the tragedy.

Nor was he ever to be concerned, save as it reflected on the skill and reputation of the one officer most involved. Almost a full year and a half later, from his Headquarters in Australia, he gave out a single formal statement. It began:

"My attention has been called to a number of statements implying criticism of the handling of the Air Forces by their Commander, Major General Lewis H. Brereton, in the Philippines at the beginning of the war, the implication being that through neglect or faulty judgment he failed to take proper security measures, resulting in the destruction of his Air Force on the ground. Such statements do grave injustice to this officer and his gallant subordinates. General Brereton had in the Philippines only a token force which, excluding trainers and hopelessly obsolete planes, comprised but thirty-five heavy bombers and seventy-two fighters. He was further greatly handicapped by the lack of airdromes, there being only one in Luzon, Clark Field, that was usable for heavy bombers and only five usable by fighters. . . . The Air Forces in the Philippines planned carefully and executed valiantly. Any attempt to decry their record can spring only from a complete lack of knowledge of the facts involved."

It was a magnanimous gesture by a commander who was ready to take the blame for any defeat in his theater, and ready, as well, to give the credit for victory to others. But his refusal to punish the guilty subordinates who in the hot fury of war made mistakes, brought on MacArthur the ceaseless criticism of bitter men who have wanted only to humiliate and destroy him personally.

* * * *

Joe Stevenot and his telephone girls and watchers were busy with rumors and ghost stories during these swift-ticking hours that followed the first bombings. Wild tales sung over the wires, and MacArthur and his staff spent more than a little of their time evaluating these rumors, trying to sift the grains of truth from the mass of chaff.

It was evident that the enemy was determined to clear the air of defending planes, and if possible knock out the more important flying fields in central Luzon. Shortly after the disastrous raid on Clark Field, a second formation of fifty-four Jap bombers and a great mass of dive bombers attacked the field and installations in Iba, on the China Sea, some twenty-five or thirty miles over the mountains directly west of Clark Field. Nichols Field, on the outskirts of Manila, was yet to be bombed, but its time would come soon enough.

Systematically the enemy went about his job of air destruction. His tactics were superb in their cunning. He would send in several formations of bombers and fighters, lure the handful of defending pursuit ships from their fields, keep them in the air until they were out of gas and were forced to come down. Then he would pounce down on them with his fresh, inexhaustible reserve echelons for the kill. With his overwhelming superiority of air mass the plan was unbeatable.

No fighters ever struck back with more energy and valor than did the little band of American and Filipino pilots. Within calling distance the Japanese had between two and three thousand planes. At any moment and at any point they chose they could send in an overwhelmingly superior air force. They outnumbered the defenders not less than thirty to one in immediate resources available.

It was a foregone conclusion to MacArthur that his slender air forces would soon be whittled down to little or nothing. Yet he had a vast coastline to watch and deny to the enemy on Luzon Island alone. His remaining bombers flew up from Mindanao singly and in pairs on their reconnaissance missions. They could help deny the beaches, but he was certain that the Japanese would soon begin their landings.

Just before dawn on December 10th a message came through that the Japanese had captured a beach-head at Vigan on the China Sea, almost 250 miles north of Manila, and some hundred miles above the great Lingayen Gulf, where ultimately Jap landings were certain to be made. A scout-car platoon of the 26th Cavalry had run into the landing at Vigan, and had been lucky to get out with its cars and report the grave news to Headquarters. Two hours after daylight eight American light bombers attacked the Japanese ships at low altitude. The damage they did was well worth the loss of five of the eight planes.

All that day and the following the Japs continued their air attacks, smashing fields and installations. At dawn on the 12th the Japs landed at Legaspi at the very bottom of Luzon Island, a port almost as far southeast of Manila as Vigan was to the north. A second northern landing had already been made at Aparri, at the extreme northern end of the Island. Here, and at the other two landing spots, were air strips that could be used as staging fields for Jap fighter craft.

To MacArthur's professional eyes the pattern was developing exactly as he had expected. The Japanese first knocked out most of the defending air force, and secured beach-heads in both the extreme north and the south of Luzon. MacArthur was certain neither of these would be the main beach-head, and he refused to have his meager defending forces thrown out of kilter to meet these feints. He was still positive that the real Jap attempts would be made on Lingayen Gulf, on the China Sea, a hundred and twenty miles north of Manila, and at Lamon Bay, on the Pacific Ocean side, a scant sixty miles southeast of Manila. Here at Lamon Bay the queer-shaped island of Luzon was pinched into a narrow neck of land, less than ten miles wide. Below this, to the southeastward, stretched almost two hundred more miles of country, ending with the town of Legaspi, now in Jap hands.

On December 12th, the same day the Japs landed at Legaspi, they attempted to force a beach-head on vital Lingayen Gulf, far to the north. Here they were bloodily repulsed, losing at least two of their twelve transports from air bombs and shore batteries. It was a definite failure, and besides it tipped their hand. Lingayen certainly would be the real point of attack. Long before this MacArthur had massed some of his best units here. He was ready.

Even with the natural confusion and upset of war, the rate of final mobilization of the Philippine Army was being accelerated. Infantry regiments from two of the southern islands' divisions were ferried to Luzon and put into position. All busses and automobiles were pressed into service, so that troops could be moved swiftly. It was to be one of the telling factors in carrying out the subsequent strategy.

Doubting Thomases, who had said that Filipinos would not throw themselves into the war, were to have their eyes opened by a sudden out-flowing of patriotism. The Filipinos gladly put their all into the struggle. Men and women alike willingly made every sacrifice. A brave and loyal people arose, determined to fight for their country; in spirit, it was another Russia at war.

Hideous days of bombing followed nights of uncertainty. Then at dawn on December 22nd, eighty Japanese transports steamed into Lingayen Gulf, north of Manila on the China Sea—and the great invasion was on. With superb skill every landing was beaten off, save the one made at Agoo. Here the exhausted defenders were suddenly struck on their right flank by a body of the enemy that had worked its way southward from the initial landing at Vigan. The defenders were forced back, and at San Carlos they made their stand. But many thousands of Japanese troops had now landed and were hurried into position. There had been little air opposition, and the defending forces were meager.

Simultaneous with the heavy landings on Lingayen, the Japs sent forty transports into Lamon Bay, to the south of Manila, at the narrowest point of the peninsula. Quickly they poured thousands of troops into the beach-head they already held at Atimonan. But already those good old Manila busses were roaring up from the south, bringing out the soldiers that would be trapped below, once the heavy Japanese force cut the narrow peninsula.

The battle was joined both on the north and the south. The great Jap prongs now moved towards the restricted Manila area, each attempting to drive the converging defending forces together and prevent their retirement to Bataan.

Rapidly pushing straight eastward across central Luzon from Lingayen Bay, a heavy Japanese force soon contacted a second Japanese army that had come down the Cagayan Valley from Aparri, in the far north. These combined Japanese forces in the north had no less than five complete infantry divisions, with a brigade of tanks, and other supporting troops. For months they had been specially trained in Formosa and in China. They were the cream of the Japanese Army.

Against them MacArthur had his hastily organized and incomplete First Philippine Division, with its American and Philippine Scout units; and his partially trained, half-equipped infantry regiments of three Philippine divisions, supported by certain artillery units. Already in the Cagayan Valley, the brilliant 26th Cavalry regiment of the Philippine Scouts had played a heroic role of defense; they were to be helped by a rag, tag and bobtail bunch of American and Philippine mining engineers and demolition experts, whose story reads almost like a fantastic Alice in Wonderland epic of war.

Early in October, General MacArthur had requested the War Department to send out by China Clipper a certain stocky, wide-eyed, West Point graduate, a Lt. Col. of Engineers, named Hugh Casey. He had worked before for the Military Mission here in the Philippines. As an Army engineering consultant, he had laid out the plans for great hydro-electric plants, bridges and dams, that were to be a part of the grand over-all planning scheme of Philippine defense and independence.

He had little more than arrived in the Islands this second time when it became clear that at any moment war might break out. MacArthur sent for him at once. Casey was told to form a makeshift army engineering outfit, and to retard in every possible way the advance of enemy troops. If necessary he was to scorch-earth everything of military value that might fall into the hands of the enemy. That was all. He could work out his own details and methods. That was the way MacArthur delegated authority. He had been an Engineer officer himself and he knew demolitions thoroughly and their great possibilities, and what was more he knew Casey.

Casey went to work. In the years he had spent as an Army Engineer in the Islands, he had met most of the civilian engineers there, both American and Filipino. For the immediate job at hand he would need the tough, imaginative and resourceful mining engineers who had been opening up the gold properties in central Luzon. He hurriedly sent for these rugged representatives of this hard breed. Casey quickly interviewed them, tossed them Army commissions, and laid out their jobs. Each man was to get together his own gang of dynamiters. Already Casey had grabbed all the explosives there were in the Island, and put them in a great pool. Fortunately a shipload of high explosives had arrived only a day or two before war came. This was worth its weight in pure gold to Casey's Wreckers.

Without delay the fighting engineer sent his demolition gangs north and south to all key road and bridge positions. As the Japs massed their two overpowering forces—one in the north of Manila and the second in the south—Casey's men joined up with the defending rear guard outfits, and placed themselves under the local senior officer. It was a strange little army, with its catch-as-catch-can trucks and cars of dynamite and fuses, its booted, bearded old miners and their loyal native helpers. Men who work deep under the earth are fearless men. They live precariously and die bravely. These were Casey's Dynamiters.

It was perfectly clear in MacArthur's mind that the forces he had at hand could not possibly stand against the overwhelming weight of the highly trained, perfectly weaponed and coordinated army of invaders. The enemy had absolute control of the air and the sea approaches.

At best MacArthur could fight only a delaying action, holding back these crushing jaws of the pincers, until he could move his troops up from the south, push them through the bottleneck of Manila, and cross the wide Calumit bridge over the Pampanga River. From this key junction, forty miles north of the capital, his soldiers and their scanty equipment could be side-slipped west into the jungles and mountains of Bataan Peninsula. It was a delicate operation at best, with the odds all against him. Its success would depend basically upon his own skill.

To execute successfully this great withdrawal, his covering forces in the north would have to hold back the Japs spewing by the thousands out of the widening beach-heads in Lingayen Gulf southward down the central plain of Luzon. It was largely a matter of timing. A wrong move, a single miscalculation, and disaster would follow. If this northern Japanese army broke through, captured this key Calumit bridge over the Pampanga River, before the southern defending forces could go over it, then

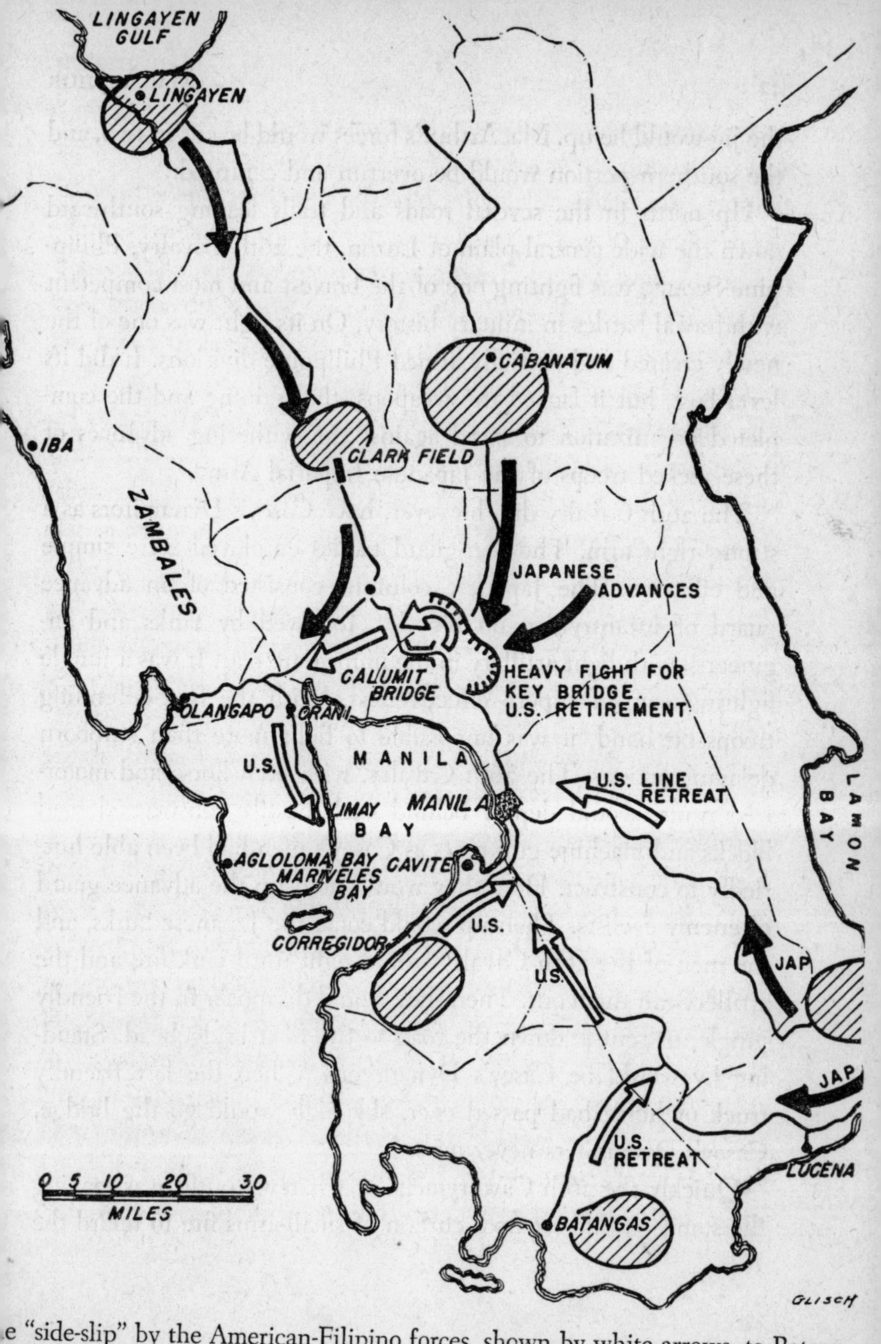

e "side-slip" by the American-Filipino forces, shown by white arrows, to Bataan. Calumit bridge, above Manila, was the key to the successful withdrawal.

the jig would be up. MacArthur's forces would be cut in two, and the southern portion would be overrun and captured.

Up north in the several roads and trails leading southward down the wide central plain of Luzon, the 26th Cavalry, Philippine Scouts, was fighting one of the bravest and most competent withdrawal battles in military history. On its right was one of the newly created and partially armed Philippine divisions. It did its level best, but it lacked the weapons, the training and the completed organization to stand against the withering advances of these picked troops of the Japanese Imperial Army.

The 26th Cavalry did, however, have Casey's Dynamiters as a strong right arm. The rear-guard tactics employed were simple and effective. The Japanese columns consisted of an advance guard of infantrymen on bicycles, followed by tanks and engineers—with light artillery in the immediate rear. It was a jungle fighting-team of superb effectiveness. With the few defending troops on hand, it was impossible to fight more than stubborn delaying actions. The 26th Cavalry, with both horse and motorized units, would deploy behind such hastily constructed road blocks and machine gun nests as Casey's men had been able hurriedly to construct. Here they would hold up the advance guard of enemy cyclists. Then up would come the Japanese tanks, and the men of the 26th Cavalry would fight until tank fire and the artillery ran them out. Then they would disappear in the friendly jungle, or scuttle down the road to the next bridgehead. Standing by would be Casey's Dynamiters. When the last friendly truck or horse had passed over, sky high would go the bridge. Casey's Dynamiters never missed.

Quickly the 26th Cavalrymen—or whatever outfit was making the stand—would set up a curtain of small-arms fire to retard the

enemy. Eventually the enemy tanks would drive t
his engineers were hurried up and repaired the
while far down the road, on to the south, Casey
be constructing new defense positions near the ne
pounding in their charges of explosives for a repetition of the
deadly delaying tactics.

Back in Manila there was tenseness and worry. Long ago the great naval base at Cavite, around the bend of the Bay from the capital, had been bombed to death. Admiral Hart had ordered his surface fleet to the south, to join up with the Dutch, where matters were quickly going from bad to worse. Even his twenty-seven submarines were sent away. Thirty-mile-wide Manila Bay was dangerous to surface warships, but it was a gloomy, sad day for those who stayed behind to watch the little American Asiatic Fleet slip away in the gathering darkness.

On the land, although things were running against him, MacArthur had anticipated every enemy move. Manila, obviously, was doomed. Yet it might still be saved from actual physical destruction. He could move the military out and then declare it an open city. He could spare it—this city he loved so well—if he could act in time. He would set up GHQ at Corregidor, the only place outside of Manila which could maintain radio communication with Washington and the outside world. He would take the civil government with him—both Quezon and Sayre—and he would transfer the Philippine gold reserve with them. All this was quietly done on Christmas Eve.

Washington sent word he was to resume his rank of full General, which put him back in the place he held so long as the senior line officer of the Army. He was fully satisfied with the y the fighting had gone so far. His green and poorly armed troops had done splendid work. He was sure he could successfully direct and time his great twin withdrawals into the mountain fastness of Bataan.

But distressing news was coming in from the outside world. On Christmas Day the great British base at Hong Kong fell. And there was nothing but disturbing word concerning the Japanese campaign that aimed at cleaning up the Malayan Peninsula, and then driving straight at Singapore. Things were going bad everywhere outside.

In the north our defending forces were beginning to crumble before overwhelming odds. At points the enemy's penetrations were endangering the entire line of defense. In the south, below Manila, there were still thousands of troops, guns and equipment to get through the bottleneck of Manila, over that key Calumit bridge, and into the safety of Bataan.

Suddenly the situation became dangerous. A Japanese column had broken through the road defenses on the east of the Central Luzon plain. It was moving swiftly towards the Calumit bridge. At 7:30 on the evening of December 28th more disturbing reports came. Only a miracle could save the bridge and the regiments moving up from Manila and the south.

MacArthur acted instantly. A battalion of tanks was moving up with the converging southern groups. Two batteries of self-propelled three-inch guns were off to the west. These outfits and all other available troops were ordered to push at top speed to this critical road area. There was no moment to lose. The orders were peremptory. The road at Balinaug must be blocked. There must be a stand to the death made here.

All the early hours of the night the tank units and self-propelled artillery batteries and the trucks with troops and ammunition roared north. MacArthur calmly studied the reports until two o'clock in the morning. Then he turned to Sutherland, his Chief of Staff: "That'll do it, Dick," he pronounced with confidence—then he went to bed.

At daybreak the enemy column smashed into the unexpected defense. It was stopped in its tracks. The fighting was heavy and crucial. Again and again the Japanese attacked. Always they were checked.

All that day trucks and busses and motor cars streamed across the vital bridge. Then slowly the holding troops gave way. Casey's Dynamiters blew a remaining little bridge in front of the Japanese advance late New Year's Eve, and the covering force made its final retirement. At three o'clock New Year's Day the last weary and hungry soldier, the last gun carriage and tired truck safely crossed the great Calumit bridge.

Casey's Dynamiters had carefully placed their heavy charges. At dawn that New Year's Day of 1942, the advance guard of the enemy columns cautiously started across the great steel and concrete structure. Casey's men waited until they were half way over, then they slammed down the switches. There was no Jap left to tell the tale.

The southern forces of MacArthur's army had been saved. They could now take up positions on Bataan.

The far-flung battles for the beaches and roads and river bridges were over now. It had been a skillful withdrawal. MacArthur's timing had been perfect. His entire forces were set in their final positions.

Here in the mountain jungle and green forests of rugged Bataan Peninsula, he would fight the good fight; and on the barren Rock of Corregidor, there would be great loneliness and hours of anguish and uncertainty for him.

CHAPTER FOUR

THE Rock had had its first really heavy bombing on December 29th. The General and his family were ensconced on Top Side, in what had been the home of Major General George Moore, Commander of Corregidor Garrison. The island fortress is shaped like a pollywog. Top Side 600 feet high is the head of the pollywog. The head, some two miles in diameter, faces west into the China Sea; the tail, some three miles long, points east toward Manila. Middle Side, with its great barracks and storehouses, is part way down toward the neck; Bottom Side is the low neck which connects the head to the long, curving rocky tail of the pollywog. Just below the neck a rock hill rises 300 feet above the sea. Straight through this hill a tunnel had been cut years before by native convict laborers, loaned to the army. There had been no appropriation available, so the 800 prisoners on hand had been put to work. Before the job was done a tunnel some 600 feet long had been cut out of the solid rock, and rock rooms carved out at right angles. A street-car track ran straight through it. Foul as the air inside soon became, it was to prove a haven and a godsend to weary, exhausted men and women.

At 11:41, on December 29th, a great formation of enemy bombers, flying high, came over the Rock. The General stepped out into the narrow lawn in front of his house on Top Side. He suggested to Mrs. MacArthur that she take Arthur and the Chinese nurse to a long, narrow dugout, a few hundred feet away, that served as a communications center and telephone

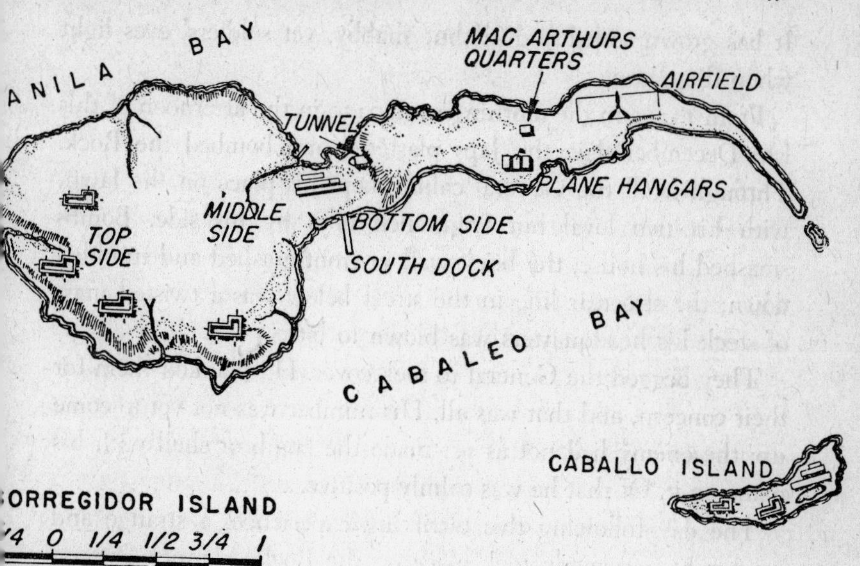

MacArthur's Headquarters was originally on Top Side: but after the heavy mbing of Dec. 29, he was forced to move to the lower end of the queer-shaped tress.

exchange. There would at least be safety here from bomb splinters, and only a direct hit need be feared.

The General stayed behind with his Filipino driver and orderly to watch the bombing. One of the boys tried to give him a steel helmet, but the General refused. He was wearing the heavily gold-embroidered cap that had been made for him in Washington. It was to become famous throughout the Army. Later it was to see the General through the hard and desperate days on New Guinea. It was to head the line of the paratroops when they closed the ring at Lae. Under snipers' fire in the brilliant landing on the Admiralty Islands it was to lead the way.

It has grown soiled and all but shabby, yet soldiers' eyes light when they see it.

From 11:41 in the morning until 2:30 in the afternoon of this late December day, the Japs plastered and bombed the Rock. Through it all the General calmly kept his place on the lawn, with his two loyal but frightened boys by his side. Bombs smashed his house; the brick wall in front crashed and tumbled down; the streetcar line in the street below was a twisted mass of steel; his headquarters was blown to bits.

They begged the General to seek cover. He thanked them for their concern, and that was all. His number was not yet to come up; the enemy had not as yet made the bomb or shell with his name on it. Of that he was calmly positive.

The day following this terrifying experience, a strange and memorable ceremony took place on the Rock. Manuel Quezon was for the second time formally inaugurated as President of the Philippine Commonwealth. It was in direct contrast to the magnificence and color of the first inaugural, when the Vice President of the United States and a great party from Washington attended.

This time it was a small and solemn gathering. The All Clear had sounded and the party gathered quietly and a little hurriedly. President Quezon and High Commissioner Sayre each spoke feelingly and with deep meaning. Then MacArthur spoke. His voice carried hardly to the edge of the little gathering:

"Never before in all history has there been a more solemn and significant inauguration. An act, symbolical of democratic processes, is placed against the background of a sudden, merciless war.

"The thunder of death and destruction, dropped from the skies, can be heard in the distance. Our ears almost catch the roar of battle as our soldiers close on the firing line. The horizon is blackened by the smoke of destructive fire. The air reverberates to the dull roar of exploding bombs.

"Such is the bed of birth of this new government, of this new nation. For four hundred years the Philippines have struggled upward toward self-government. Just at the end of its tuitionary period, just on the threshold of independence, came the great hour of decision. There was no hesitation, no vacillation, no moment of doubt. The whole country followed its great leader in choosing the side of freedom against the side of slavery. We have just inaugurated him, we have just thereby confirmed his momentous decision. Hand in hand with the United States and the other free nations of the world, this basic and fundamental issue will be fought through to victory. Come what may, ultimate triumph will be its reward.

"Through this its gasping agony of travail, through what Winston Churchill calls 'blood and sweat and tears,' from the grim shadow of the Valley of Death, oh Merciful God, preserve this noble race."

Every day now there was bombing, and before long the Japs set up heavy, long-range rifles on the mainland above Cavite, and began daily shelling from there. The damage grew. Life was harsh and brutal. Soldiers and leathernecks of the famous old 4th Regiment of Marines manned guns and fought stubbornly and bravely.

The food situation was already becoming serious. Several thousand Filipino civilians had followed the troops into the

Bataan Peninsula. This meant that there would obviously be many more mouths to feed than had been anticipated. On full rations, with three meals a day, the food supplies would last a bare three months. Fortunately there was an ample supply of ammunition: it was food that was the critical item.

"We will immediately go on half rations," the General ordered. "Serve breakfast and supper, and cut the full ration exactly in half."

Six weeks later the General ordered the ration reduced to a third of its normal size; to a scant 500 calories instead of the usual 1500 calories. It was meager and insufficient, but it would still hold soul and body together. Men of indomitable spirit could still fight on it. And fight they did.

January 2nd the advance guard of the Jap southern invasion forces cautiously entered the city of Manila. There was no resistance anywhere in the sprawling capital; it was an open city. But the invaders closed in with harshness and cruelty.

Their northern forces were now in contact with the right flank of the defending troops on Bataan. On the 5th a sharp attack was launched by the Japanese in an effort to capture the terminus of the railroad northwest from Manila. Yards here were crowded with freight cars loaded with supplies. It was a brisk and determined attack, but the invaders suffered a real repulse. Several hundred enemy were killed, and the invaders were set back on their heels. Most of the supplies piled up here were hurriedly transported to Bataan by truck and the last of our troops took up their positions there. The Japanese commander prepared for his first real assault on Bataan itself.

Bataan Peninsula is a heavily wooded, mountainous arm of land, jutting out to the south from the Luzon mainland, and forming the western shoreline of circular Manila Bay. It is roughly 15 miles wide, east and west, and between 25 and 30 miles long, north and south. In the very center of the southern half of the peninsula rises Mt. Mariveles, 4,700 feet high. In almost the exact center of the northern half, there are the twin heights of Mt. Natib and Bataan Heights. All these three elevations were of very great value to the defending forces as artillery spotting posts, in the early days of the fighting. Here MacArthur planted a number of the old First World War six-inch guns that had originally been sent over to be mounted at points guarding the Inland Sea. There had not been time to set them up, and now in the rugged defenses of beleaguered Bataan they were to prove of great value in helping to break up the early Japanese assaults.

From the beginning MacArthur's Bataan plan was to hold a line on the north that more or less paralleled the road running directly west and east across the top of the peninsula from the port of Olongapo, on Subic Bay, to Orani on the Manila Bay side. To the north of this there was tropical jungle, with rice paddies here and there cut out of the heavy forests and hillsides.

With the greater portion of his forces made up of green, inexperienced native troops, MacArthur planned on a defense in depth. His less experienced native outfits were placed in the front line positions, and behind these, for a depth of five miles and more, came a series of prepared defense positions. His most experienced and better armed units, he kept back as reserves.

The peninsula was roughly divided throughout its length into two Corps areas—one on the eastern half and one on the western half. The country between was rough and mountainous with only one or two trails and dirt roads connecting the two areas.

In final reserve in each area he held a mobile regiment of the well-trained Philippine Scouts—with the fine old 31st U. S. Infantry well back, ready to be thrown in to the support of either. MacArthur could last only as long as his reserves held out, and he was perfectly aware that each successive Japanese onslaught that he drove back, mathematically whittled down these reserves. In the end he would have none for counter-attack. The issue would then be out of his hands.

Early in January the Japanese set themselves for their first heavy assault. The unsuccessful engagement of January 5th had made them a little wary, but they were eager to try an all-out assault. The reports of Colonel Charles Willoughby, MacArthur's Intelligence head, indicated the offensive would open either January 11th or 12th.

At dawn on January 10th MacArthur crossed over by PT boat from the Rock to the little Bataan port of Mariveles. Light was just breaking when he arrived and set out for the front. The rough roads were six inches deep in soft dirt. Dust and steaming heat were everywhere.

Steady artillery firing was going on. Overhead the Dawn Patrol of the Japanese was making its usual call. Trucks and Manila busses, bearing troops and supplies, were sending up those endless streams of dust that in a weird way hung like gaunt, gray ribbons high in the sky above the dirt trails.

All day long MacArthur made his way from one division Command Post to another. By car and on foot he visited regimental headquarters, battery stations and battalion CP's. He followed narrow trails to front lines and chatted with tall lean sergeants from Texas and Illinois, and slender little native boys from lower Luzon. Everywhere he left a feeling of strength and sureness.

There would be no giving way. The Jap must not only be stopped but defeated and pushed back. Help from the outside was to come before long. Nothing could be more certain than that. In the meantime they must hold on—stop the Japanese and drive him back.

Not even the field hospitals and advance dressing stations were overlooked. Brave, tireless nurses, worn out by the bombers and the streams of wounded men they struggled so hard to save, found encouragement in his words of praise. Under his inspiration the spirit of a whole army—a beaten and hungry army—rose like a bright morning sun. It came at exactly the moment when it was most needed. Forty-eight hours later, the Japanese struck with all the fury they possessed.

The well-trained enemy forces broke through the first line on the defenders' right flank. It was a moment of great danger. MacArthur waited until the enemy had expended himself, then he ordered the Philippine Scouts to counter-attack. Staggering under the heavy blows, the Japanese gave ground. They were hurled back to their original position, and still the counter-attack pushed them on. When darkness came, the American-Filipino forces were from one to two miles beyond the original Japanese lines.

If at this moment MacArthur had had sufficient fresh troops he might have achieved a complete victory, for the enemy had received a very bloody nose. The Japanese had been roundly whipped. They had lost heavily and had been humiliated. It was clear that they must bring up heavy reinforcements, new tank units and bigger guns, before they could dare try their luck again.

Two weeks later the Japanese made their second big attempt. This time they laid down an eight-hour artillery preparation.

Then the barrage lifted and the enemy again drove a strong wedge into the defenders' right flank. His tank units and infantry now pushed down the road that bordered the eastern shore line. The whole American-Filipino right flank was in grave danger of being turned by this deep salient. It was a critical moment.

MacArthur bided his time. When the exact moment came, he shot in his best troops against the deep but thin enemy wedge, cut through it and once again the Jap invaders were swept back to their jumping-off point. It was a master counterattack perfectly timed and executed. For the next forty-eight hours MacArthur continued to stab and jab at the enemy. Not for days to come were the Japanese able to pull themselves together to launch a fresh attack here on the right. But in the end MacArthur's forces had so dwindled that fresh assaults were no longer justified. They could only settle back to meet the Japanese onslaughts which soon were being stubbornly pressed.

Across the peninsula to the west on the left flank the defense lines were not continuous. MacArthur held the port of Olongapo, in Subic Bay, at the extreme northwest corner of Bataan. He had held such mobile reserves as were available there in position to prevent isolation of the Olongapo garrison.

One dawn early in January the Japanese attempted a surprise landing below and behind our Olongapo position. These were tactics they had been successfuly using against the British in Malaya. But here in rugged Bataan they were to find MacArthur prepared and alert to the dangers of their enveloping landings.

Defending troops were immediately thrown in to meet the dangerous flank attack from the sea. There was hand-to-hand fighting, but in the end every Japanese who had landed was killed. But in wiping out this dangerous landing the American-

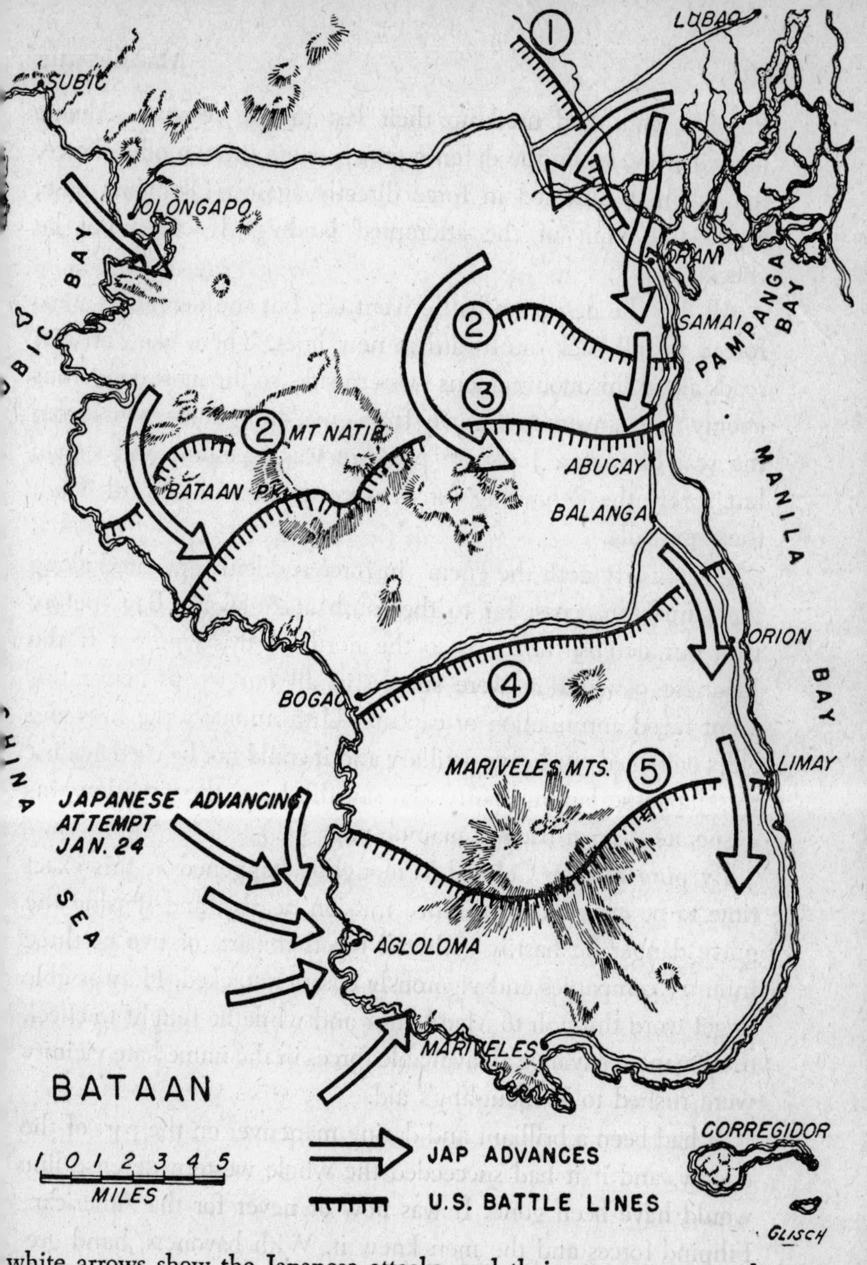

white arrows show the Japanese attacks, and their attempts at envelopment and infiltration from the China Sea side.

Filipino units had used up their last mobile reserves. Almost immediately, while the defense groups were thrown off balance, the Japanese attacked in force directly against Olongapo base, above the point of the attempted landing. It could not be checked.

All day the desperate battle went on, but the defenders were forced to fall back southward to new lines. There were no real roads along this mountainous western side, so the most dangerous enemy threats were necessarily from enveloping movements from the sea. However, Japanese pressure was incessant and slowly but surely the defending forces were pushed southward down the peninsula.

On January 20th the enemy in force suddenly appeared along the China Sea coast far to the south at Agloloma Bay. Before this, our defense line was to the north of this landing. If the Japanese penetration were successful all our troops above this point faced annihilation or capture. Unfortunately the hills and cliffs defiladed our heavy artillery and it could not be used against this Japanese landing party. To say the least, the situation was desperate. (Turn back to map on page 55.)

By pure chance Colonel Willoughby happened at this exact time to be on a reconnaissance mission nearby, and sensing the grave danger he hastily gathered together parts of two or three infantry companies and vigorously counterattacked. He was able to get word through to MacArthur and while he fought to check the Japanese advance all available forces in the immediate vicinity were rushed to Willoughby's aid.

It had been a brilliant and daring maneuver on the part of the enemy, and if it had succeeded the whole western defense line would have been gone. It was now or never for the American-Filipino forces and the men knew it. With bayonets, hand grenades and submachine-gun fire they drove back the Japanese, over the cliffs and on into the sea. Of such stuff are heroes made.

This desperate landing attempt at Agloloma Bay was only one of a series of such enveloping movements from the China Sea. The Japanese had complete control of both the sea and the air, and they had the landing craft and barges to make surprise landings on almost any beach-head or river mouth they chose.

Meanwhile on the eastern side of Bataan, along Manila Bay, there were likewise days and nights of bitter fighting. Then suddenly there would be a blessed respite, and while the Japanese were bringing up new reinforcements the fighting would settle down to artillery duels. But there was no letup on the deadly attacks by the Japanese bombers and dive bombers, eternally searching out the hidden gun positions.

* * * *

On Corregidor, blasted daily by bombs, MacArthur was not only worried about our own desperate situation but he watched with heavy heart the disastrous turn of events in British Malaya. The native peoples of this part of the world were making little or no effective effort to help their white masters in the hour of peril. Only in the Philippines were the natives loyal and eager to fight and die. Here the contacts between two nations had been so fair and honest that there was real brotherhood and mutual loyalty. Forty years of American-Philippine relationship based on justice and right was now to show a thoughtless world what could be done when the heart was pure.

On January 31st word came that the last of the British forces had been overrun in the once heavily held Malayan peninsula. Only the vast fortress of Singapore still remained to be captured. British leaders long before had pledged Washington that Singapore and Malaya could hold indefinitely, and be kept as a base for operations to relieve the Philippines. This guarantee unquestionably had much weight in the grave decision to throw the whole might of American arms into the European scene, at the almost complete neglect of American honor and duty in the Philippines. And now Malaya had been overrun and lost. The mighty bastion of imperial power in Singapore Island was about to fall.

Day after day quiet drama was being enacted on the bomb-battered installations and within the foul-aired tunnel of the Rock. From the start MacArthur had flatly refused to sleep in the vast ghost-like, bomb-proof mountain shelter. When the home on Top Side had been bombed to rubble, he and Mrs. MacArthur had chosen a small house on the tail of the island about half a mile east of headquarters in the tunnel. Here he ate his two meager meals daily; here he held many of his conferences. Actual GHQ was inside the tunnel, but the General stubbornly remained outside even during the incessant air alarms and raids. Quezon protested at his unnecessary exposure. The General smiled his rare, grim smile and said quizzically, "Mr. President, some believe that dead generals are more valuable than live ones." The President never knew just what he meant. But the bomb or shell with his name on it never came over.

It was evident to MacArthur that the constant bombing and artillery fire was swiftly undermining the already delicate health of the worried President. There could be little doubt that the weight of approaching disaster was slowly killing him. Some way or other had to be found to take him to the quiet and safety of another island. The General insisted that he go, and he arranged for an American submarine to transport him there.

High Commissioner Sayre and his family and staff would go

to Australia and thence home. They had done their work and MacArthur felt they should go. The gracious Mrs. Quezon suggested to the General's wife that she and four-year-old Arthur accompany them. Mrs. MacArthur did not even talk to the General about it. She thanked Donna Aurora, then firmly announced that they would remain behind with the General. "We three drink of the same cup," she said simply.

Darkness had covered the beleaguered Rock where the General half-carried the aging, sick President from his car to the gangplank, where the submarine awaited them. Tears were in the eyes of both men when they said goodbye. The submarine slowly disappeared in the gathering darkness and the General returned to his quarters. He was still calm and determined, but he was beginning to look to the east for the help that was never to come.

His code dispatches to Washington had long before given complete details and plans of the secret airfields and strips for fighters that might be flown in from carriers and then sent on northward from Mindanao. In anticipation of help airfield construction continued by our engineers until April.

A bomber and air transport route all the way from Australia was still open and usable. There was little doubt that aircraft carriers could readily steam within 500 miles of Mindanao, shoot off their fighters, and the planes work their way by the secret air strips up to Bataan. These were all practicable plans that came from the General's mind. His position was becoming perilous, and he could not understand why no word reached him of an attempt at relief.

Flowing eastward from the States were streams of planes and ships, men and supplies, all heading across the Atlantic for the distant European theater. Convoys bound for Murmansk, North Russia, lost up to 80 percent of their ships. Yet they continued to be sent. There was no dearth of courage or paucity of enterprise there in the Atlantic. Surely American responsibility to the Philippines would not be totally ignored merely because the odds were heavy and the enterprise bold and dangerous?

It was fortunate that the Japanese were now jamming the air whenever American broadcasts gave out their glowing reports of the mighty output of American factories; of the thousands of planes and tanks and guns being built; of ships and men-of-war sliding down the ways in a score of great shipyards. Only once or twice was a feeble effort made from Australia to run the blockade to Bataan with supplies, but no ship ever reached there.

As the American air armadas flew eastward through the mists and uncertainties of the North Atlantic, it became a grim joke for the men on Bataan and Corregidor to say: "They're pulling a Corrigan on us. They're heading the wrong way." And when the broadcast came that the west coast had been shelled by an enemy submarine, MacArthur with acid humor turned to his Chief of Staff and said, "Dick, you might wire them that if they will hold on for a month we will bring them help." The grapevine carried his words to the men in the foxholes and the battery pits, and that night they roared their laughter. Men about to die in battle are like that.

Morale at times was endangered. In one low period, way back in middle January, MacArthur had felt the necessity of giving out a statement for the men to hold on, that help would be coming soon. It had been of immense value. Senior officers were spending no small part of their time assuring their tired, discouraged troops that America certainly would not fail them.

Nowhere else but here were Americans being actually attacked, their sovereignty invaded, their flag dragged in the dust and fouled. Surely there would be some effort made to send help, no matter how forlorn or desperate it might be. Never for a moment would MacArthur admit there was even a possibility otherwise.

February 15th was marked in black letters on all the calendars on the Rock. The mighty fortress of Singapore fell that day. And on to the southward the defenders of the Netherlands Indies were being beaten down and overwhelmed. Defeat there seemed inevitable.

The Jap pattern of conquest was clear. The fighter-protected bombers would sweep in, destroy defending planes and air installations. Then would come the warships, and the sea would be swept clean of all surface resistance. Then key points and landing beaches would be captured. Again the bombers would sweep in, advanced bomber strips would be secured, more sea rendered safe, more bases extended.

Nowhere from Hong Kong to the shores of Australia were the native people materially to help in the defenses. Only here in the Philippines was there the true will of all to fight on. Only here in these forlorn and neglected outposts of great America were twin peoples to fight grimly and stubbornly, back to back, against overwhelming odds.

* * * *

Long before these trying days of middle February, Major General Brereton had taken his dwindling force of four-engined Flying Fortresses south to Australia for necessary overhauling and repairs. The Forts had proved their worth time and again. Captain Colin Kelly, flying up from Mindanao, had alone and unaided put out of action a great Jap battleship. Other Forts had done valiant work. But Brereton's forces never returned. They were detached from MacArthur and sent to Java under the command of Wavell.

Talented Brigadier General Harold H. George, Commander of the Pursuits, had long husbanded his swiftly disappearing little group of fighters. In pairs they had harassed the enemy's landings and reconnoitered his positions; these resourceful flying men had even tied bombs on their fuselages and sunk ships. In tiny formations they had fought whole squadrons of fast Zeros and made their marks.

But always it was a helpless game. By the end of February General George could muster only two or three of his original 72 P-40's and P-35's. In addition he had the strangest air fleet that ever cut through the blue skies. It was known as the "Bamboo Fleet," because the two or three old and worn-out training and reconnaissance planes of the original Philippine Air Force that composed it, were literally tied together with bamboo and wire and glue. Yet it was a brave, unconquerable little force. Finally, there was the famous Duck. It had started out in life as a Navy plane and had been sunk unceremoniously in the Bay near Mariveles. It had been fished out, patched up and by some miracle made to fly. It was this dauntless Duck that flew the gallant Carlos Romulo from certain death at the hands of the Japs. This distinguished Filipino editor and writer had been the Voice of Freedom that three times each day carried words of hope to his beaten countrymen. Romulo along with his immediate chief, Lt. Col. Diller, head of the invaluable Public Relations Office, had kept alive and burning the deathless epic of Bataan and Corregidor for all the world to stand before in awe.

When the last plane was put out of action, MacArthur desperately pleaded for reconnaissance replacements. "Just three planes," he begged George, "so that I can see." And when he realized they would not arrive there was bitterness for the first time in his voice when he said to his staff, "You can't fight them, if you can't see them. I am now blind."

Time was crowding down on MacArthur and his men. The General still could not believe that he had been actually abandoned. For here were the reports that great masses of American troops had been landed in Ireland. Here were the stories of a bridge of bombers thrown over the three thousand miles of ocean separating North America from England. New sea fleets were taking to the waters. North Russia, at the end of a long and dangerous sea road, was receiving hundreds of shiploads of guns, tanks, planes, food and military supplies of every kind.

Brave men by the thousands were going down to the sea in ships in order that help might be taken to our Allies. Ships were sent all the way around Africa to deliver help through the distant Red Sea and Persian Gulf. American carriers boldly sailed through the sub-infested Mediterranean to run the gantlet of the land-based bombers of the Axis in Sicily, so they might fly their planes to hard-pressed British Malta. Surely they would get relief to our own men and our own brothers here in the Philippines. Surely they would not be abandoned to their fate.

* * * *

On February 23rd a messenger hurried from the code center with a secret telegram for MacArthur. He was shocked when he read it. President Roosevelt ordered him to leave Corregidor at once, and proceed to Melbourne, Australia, to assume command of the Southwest Pacific Area. He could hardly believe his eyes. It was a promotion, it was true, and a much larger and more important command. There had been rumors that a new army had been collected there for the relief of the Philippines. But he was not sure if it was anything more than pure rumor.

He paced up and down as he made his decision. For the first time in his life he would refuse to obey a lawful order. Quietly he wrote out a blunt refusal, and then called in his senior officers to explain the situation. They unanimously disagreed with him. What good would be his insubordinate message? He would get a reprimand at best and another order to obey the first order without delay. If he persisted there could be but one result. He would be directed to turn over the command and face an inevitable court-martial.

Stubbornly these trusted friends argued that obviously he had been selected to lead a rescue force back, and all begged him to go at once. The local situation was not too bad. He still had 17,000 American troops, 10,000 Scouts and 55,000 Filipinos. With care the food would last well into June. There was still ammunition available. They might well hold out until he could return.

He tore up his first reply, and on February 24th wired Washington that he had plans and commitments that would delay his departure. For the first and only time in his life he hedged. Washington replied that he should leave as soon as possible. Again he delayed. On March 10th came another peremptory order. He was urgently needed in the new command without delay.

MacArthur had no means of knowing that two days before this, the last resistance of the Dutch had collapsed. There was little or nothing now between the victory-crazed Japanese and the final Allied bastion of Australia. Matters were precarious there, for the three regular Aussie divisions were fighting in the Middle East, far away from home. There was no minimizing the desperate situation.

MacArthur still felt that the call was not one of defense but rather to head up an expedition and lead it back to Bataan. He sent for Wainwright and told him what had happened, and gave him his orders: "Hold out until I come for you." And Wainwright with tears in his eyes pledged his beloved Chief.

It was now the Ides of March. MacArthur would leave on the dark of the moon. No submarines for him. He would go roaring out.

He called in his PT commander, Lieutenant Bulkeley. Could Buck have the four PT boats that remained fully fueled and ready to depart the following night? He could. Then the start would be made without delay. The four boats would proceed by stages to the coast of Mindanao, six or seven hundred miles to the southward from the Rock. At Del Monte field, Flying Fortresses from Port Darwin airdrome would pick up the party and fly them to Australia. That bomber route was still open. Always it could have been used to fly planes to him.

Each one of the party would take a single suitcase. Nothing else. General MacArthur, his wife and boy and nurse, his Chief of Staff, Brigadier General Sutherland, Captain Ray of the Navy, Lt. Col. Sidney Huff, his aide, and Major Morhouse, Flight Surgeon, would go in the first PT boat. They would be Lieutenant Bulkeley's personal responsibility. Admiral Rockwell, the twelve remaining officers of the staff and the confidential enlisted clerk, would be split up among the three other boats. The start would be made at 7:15 that following evening, just as twilight was dropping.

It would be a perilous voyage at best. The Japanese Navy and numerous patrol boats guarded the exits from the bay. Japanese planes constantly covered the daylight skies.

His chances at best were slim. But the decision he had been forced to make had a deeper implication than even life or death. He was leaving behind the comrades he loved and trusted.

It was the hardest decision of his life. But only by going was there any hope of help for them.

CHAPTER FIVE

ONLY ONCE OR TWICE HAS MACARTHUR HIMSELF RECITED THE story of the long and perilous trip from Corregidor to Darwin. Deep and strong flows the tide of his emotions as he lives again those tragic moments.

It was seven fifteen when the General walked across his porch to where his wife was seated. "Jean," he said gently, "it is time to mount up." Quietly they went down to the South Dock where Bulkeley waited with his PT-41. Shelling had been intermittent all day in the dock area. They boarded the vessel—all but the General. He had stopped and turned to bid Corregidor his farewell.

The men on the dock stared at the lone motionless figure they knew and loved so well. In his war-worn clothes he loomed gaunt and forlorn. His eyes roved the desperate scene before him in all its naked bleakness. Almost every building, every shed, every tree had been burned and blasted. The great fires that had raged had left their black streaks from one end of the Rock to the other. Great crevasses were torn everywhere. Corregidor looked like a tortured body that had been ripped and gouged and twisted into something no longer human.

His eyes seemed to search through the broken, shattered ruins up to the top where he could still catch the gleam of the barrels of the big guns. Up there in command of Top Side was his classmate, Paul Bunker. Forty years ago they had been associated together on one of West Point's most famous football teams—Bunker, the star, a double All American—MacArthur in the more humble role of team manager!

It was just dusk and the faint night breeze was beginning to ripple the waters. A strange silence had fallen as though death were passing by. Even the firing had ceased.

Slowly the General raised his cap—that famous cap. Even through his tan he looked white and ashen and there was the suspicion of a twitch at the muscles of his mouth. One could have heard a pin drop.

He looked around as he stepped aboard. Every man on the dock stood bareheaded. They all knew he had not more than one chance in ten.

Then came the General's quiet voice—"Cast off, Buck."

At 8:30 the four boats rendezvoused at the opening to the mine field. They crept through, led by a navy mine layer. At 9:15 they opened up the throttles and roared away.

Very shortly they began to pick up Japanese signal fires. All along the coast the enemy had established a system of signalling by fire that might have been old Indian signals. The warning signals could now clearly be seen, but the sound of the PT engines was like the sound of bombers, and the watcher mistook it.

The PT boats ran in a diamond formation, and the orders were to attack anything that blocked the way. Each of the boats carried torpedoes and 50-caliber machine guns, and the General felt they could break through any ordinary blockading line. If they were attacked from the air they were to hold together, put up a curtain of fire, and depend upon their high speed maneuverability.

Off to the left they soon made out Japanese blockading ships. Immediately they changed course to pass to the west and north. All night long similar alarms took place, but with great skill and good luck the Japanese craft were by-passed. In the diamond

pattern Bulkeley's boat led off. Admiral Rockwell in the fourth boat closed up the rear.

The seas became increasingly heavy, and the little boats pounded and rolled. It was difficult to hold formation, and about 3:30 in the morning, the pattern was broken despite every effort to hold it. They had planned to rendezvous that morning at a deserted island. When they lost formation, the lead boat tried for several hours to collect the other boats, but was unsuccessful. When day broke it headed for another deserted island, three sailing hours north of the rendezvous. Here they hoped to find cover to hide during the day.

In a distant cove they made out a small craft which was identified as one of their own ships. But those aboard failed to recognize the General's boat and prepared for conflict, dumping their spare gas drums and manning their guns. At the point of opening fire General Akin fortunately identified MacArthur's PT-boat and shouted "Hold Fire!" His keen eyesight prevented a horrible catastrophe.

They remained in the cove until about 2:30 in the afternoon, anxiously scanning the skies for the enemy's inevitable searching planes. To be spotted would be to be lost. Little Arthur was prostrated and was running a high fever. The amah was deathly sick. The General and his wife were good sailors and had weathered it well. The General ordered the vessel to try to make the original rendezvous point, a wild and uninhabited island.

The seas were running high and dangerous. The second boat had dumped its spare drums when it had mistaken MacArthur's craft for an enemy ship and its gas was running low. They found Admiral Rockwell at the rendezvous, and took on the passengers from the boat that was out of running for lack of fuel. Around

6:30 they set out to cross the Mindanao Sea for Cagayan. Rockwell's boat led and Buck's followed. The fourth boat arrived at the rendezvous about one hour after they left, and immediately followed them into the Mindanao Sea alone.

Before darkness closed in they ran into enemy destroyers, but these apparently failed to pick them up, for they slipped by them. They were getting all they could out of the old engines now. The Mindanao Sea was choppy and they were taking heavy punishment. It was like being in a cement mixer, which buffeted them from one side to the other. The next day most of the passengers were black and blue from head to foot.

It had just turned daybreak when they arrived at Cagayan in north central Mindanao. The General turned to Buck and his officers and men of the two boats. "It was done in true naval style," he gratefully pronounced. "I take great honor in awarding the boats' crews the Silver Star for gallantry and fortitude in the face of heavy odds."

General Sharp met them at the dock. He was General MacArthur's Commander in Mindanao and had a force of about 25,000 men. In the Visayas, General Chenowyth had about 20,000 men. These were units of the Philippine Army in those sectors which had been mobilized when the war broke. It had been General MacArthur's plan to use these troops in guerrilla warfare, if the defense of Bataan failed.

Four bombers had been ordered from Australia to meet the party. Two failed to arrive and the third crashed in the Bay. The fourth was so old and dilapidated that General Sharp had started it back to Australia without passengers before MacArthur's arrival.

Three replacement planes were at once started from Australia

the word: Three bombers, B-17's, were sent and arrived and departed safely. Of three sent previously with supplies, the only mission, one arrived, one crashed off Mindanao, one stopped at Dar[illegible] and two of them finally arrived. In the meantime the Japanese had word that the MacArthur staff had reached Mindanao and they rapidly pushed forces north from Davao to seize the field. The planes arrived just before midnight, and took off shortly afterwards. They were flying over enemy-held country patrolled by enemy planes, but under cover of the night they managed to evade all contacts. At 9 that morning they arrived at Batchelor Field, forty miles south of Port Darwin. "It was close," said the General on landing: "but that's the way it is in war. You win or lose, live or die—and the difference is just an eyelash."

But they still faced danger. The Japanese evidently had spotted the two planes, for in less than three hours after the Forts had landed on Batchelor Field, a heavy air attack was launched. The General's party had left for Alice Springs by a scant ten minutes when the dive bombers and fighters roared in. But the priceless quarry was gone.

Before leaving the field the General asked an American officer how many U. S. troops had been collected here in Australia for the Philippine Rescue Force.

The officer seemed bewildered and replied, "So far as I know, there are very few troops here."

MacArthur was incredulous. He turned to Dick Sutherland, his Chief of Staff, and in an aside remarked, "Surely he is wrong." It seemed impossible that the officer didn't even know about the expeditionary force he would lead back to Bataan. This rescue force was the dominant thing in the General's mind. Obviously the young officer had been marooned up in Darwin, and simply didn't know what was going on.

It was a three-hour flight to Alice Springs, where a narrow-gauge railroad dribbled southward across the endless Australian

Never-Never land. The semi-weekly train had left before the General's party arrived, but a courteous Australian camp commander arranged for a makeshift special train. It would be ready for the party immediately after lunch the following day.

It was a funny little two-coach train, and as they bumped over the white desert the General regaled his wife and the party with anecdotes of early western American travel. In one of the old wooden coaches an army field kitchen had been installed, and there were tubs of ice in lieu of a refrigerator. Two Aussie sergeants looked after the meals, and an Australian nurse helped out as best she could.

Late that afternoon they picked up a narrow-gauge sleeping car. It had been a hard and perilous journey by sea and air from Corregidor, but here was rest and peace and wonderful quiet. Despite the heat and the flies and the funny little train, it was a bit of heaven to the exhausted party. They were able to recharge their batteries, and refresh themselves.

Dick Marshall, Deputy Chief of Staff, had flown from Alice Springs to Melbourne to arrange for the arrival, and to get as much definite information as he could. He met the party on the afternoon of the third day outside Adelaide, South Australia, where the wide gauge begins. The Commissioner of Railways had placed his own private car at the General's disposal, and the party transferred from their merry little train to the luxury of this modern car.

The first question the General asked was exactly the number and disposition of the American forces here. Marshall told him the astounding truth; in the whole of Australia there was a grand total of 25,364 U. S. Army personnel, including 2,024 officers and 121 nurses. These forces comprised two Coast Artillery Regiments Antiaircraft; a regiment and one or two additional battalions of artillery; two General Service regiments of Engineers, with two extra colored battalions; some Air Corps personnel and some special troops. In the whole continent there was practically no U. S. Infantry. The Air Corps had a grand total of 250 planes more or less in commission, 65 were undergoing repairs, and 122 were under erection. The various ground and air units were scattered over an area fully as large as continental United States.

All that was blow enough, but the real alarming news Marshall brought was that, save for a single brigade of the 6th Division that had just arrived in Perth, every one of the experienced units of the Australian Imperial Force was out of the country, centered mostly in the Middle East. Australia was in dark peril. All thought of a Rescue Force for Bataan was so much blue sky beyond the horizon. It was questionable if Australia itself could be defended.

When the full force of this awful truth struck MacArthur he was stunned. He had come with the definite hope of organizing and leading an army of liberation back to the Philippines—and now he found he had no army to lead. For a moment he looked as though he had received a mortal blow. His knees seemed to buckle under him. His face was white; his lips twitched as if he were in actual pain.

It was the first time in a long life of danger and excitement on numberless battlefields that he had ever quailed. The blow seemed almost to have broken his heart. "God have mercy on us," he whispered through trembling, blanched lips. It was the cry of a tortured soul.

All that night, as the train drove through the darkness towards

Melbourne, he walked the corridor of his car alone. For hour on hour he paced up and down fighting his battle.

He was walking through the bleak cold of Valley Forge. All hope of rescuing his beloved soldiers was gone. He now faced what promised to be another losing fight—another Bataan—in this distant, isolated continent. It seemed he was once again to be defeated—once again to be the leader of a Lost Cause.

It was cold and dark as he paced the corridor. The future seemed as black as the night outside. Had fate at last betrayed him?

But when morning came he was calm and serene in the invincible dignity that was his.

He had recovered.

* * * *

It was nine o'clock when the train pulled into the station at Melbourne. MacArthur was resting on the observation platform of his car. Suddenly he realized that these cheering thousands who crowded the station platform and the street outside were greeting him.

Officials met him and escorted him from the car. A platoon of American soldiers was lined up as a Guard of Honor. There had been no U. S. infantrymen available, so a platoon of Engineers had hurriedly been brought in. A young Lieutenant brushed up their somewhat ragged Manual of Arms.

MacArthur took the salute and walked along the company front. If they had been West Point Cadets he could not have shown more pride in them. Just beyond the last file, a group of Australian and American newspapermen had gathered, and the General was asked to speak a moment to them. At breakfast on the private car it had been suggested that he would probably have to make some little statement about his arrival. He had found a folded sheet of paper and scribbled out on it a few notes. It wouldn't even faintly resemble a formal speech; he would say only what was in his heart.

As the General approached the party of newspaper men, an announcer for the Australian Broadcasting Company held up a hand microphone so that his words to the press might be broadcast. Lonely, frightened men and women on isolated farms, in distant villages and in seacoast towns and cities on this great and helpless continent below the Equator, caught the solemn words of this trusted soldier from another land . . .

"I am glad indeed to be in immediate cooperation with the Australian soldier. I know him well from World War days and admire him greatly. I have every confidence in the ultimate success of our joint cause; but success in modern war requires something more than courage and a willingness to die; it requires careful preparation. This means the furnishing of sufficient troops and sufficient material to meet the known strength of the potential enemy. No general can make something out of nothing. My success or failure will depend primarily upon the resources which the respective Governments place at my disposal. In any event I shall do my best. I shall keep the soldier's faith."

All around him men and women who were not afraid to show their emotions were cheering madly. There was a chance for Australia now.

* * * *

Four days later MacArthur and his two senior officers drove by car to the magnificent new capital at Canberra. His orders making him Supreme Commander had not as yet arrived, but he had no time to waste.

He had been told that the quiet, reserved Labor Prime Minister had been back of the original request that a Southwest Pacific theater be established, and that an American officer be placed in supreme command. Mr. Curtin had even strongly intimated that MacArthur be the man chosen for the difficult task. The inspiration of MacArthur's great fight in the Philippines had set fire to the discouraged hearts of the seven million people in this vast continent Down Under. He was the one leader they wanted. And as diplomatically as possible, Premier John Curtin had made this known to Washington.

And now MacArthur was travelling the 200 miles to Canberra to attend a meeting of the Australian War Council, and then in the evening be the guest of honor at a banquet given by the Prime Minister and the members of Parliament. Much of his ultimate success or failure would depend on the way these two momentous meetings were handled.

The Prime Minister received MacArthur alone in his office. It was a cordial, friendly talk they had. At the close the American put his hand on the shoulder of the sturdy, honest Australian.

"Mr. Prime Minister," he said solemnly, "you and I will see this through together." Curtin warmly shook his hand, and the two of them walked to the War Council meeting.

The Prime Minister introduced MacArthur to his colleagues and asked him to speak to them. He talked for more than an hour and at the end they were with him to a man. They pledged Australia to him as a unit, and to its maximum war effort.

It was a definite triumph. It was clear to these worried, harassed men that MacArthur would fight for them, that he would lead them, and that out of it somehow would come victory.

Since that day Australian leaders have been true to their pledge. They have seen it through. They have never lessened by a hair's breadth their deep and abiding belief in MacArthur and his cause.

And that first night when he appeared at this unprecedented dinner in his simple khaki battle uniform, without blouse or medals, he won the loyalty of every member of the Australian Parliament, and of the millions of plain people scattered from the busy streets of Sydney to the last lonely ranch station Back of Beyond.

He spoke slowly and in low, measured tones. His war-weary face was drawn and haggard. He talked without notes, and as the full purport of his words sank into the hearts of his listeners there was not a single dry eye in all the distinguished gathering.

It was their land, their children, their liberties, their honor, and their very hope of life that he was promising to defend. It was a warm and human declaration of faith and hope he was giving to them. . . .

"I am greatly moved by the warmth of the greeting extended to me by all of Australia. The hospitality of your country is proverbial throughout the world, but your reception has far exceeded anything that I could have anticipated.

"Although this is my first trip to Australia, I already feel at home. There is a link that binds our countries together which does not depend upon a written protocol, upon treaties of alliance, or upon diplomatic doctrine.

"It goes deeper than that. It is that indescribable consanguinity of race which causes us to have the same aspirations, the same hopes and desires, the same ideals and the same dreams of future destiny.

"My presence here is tangible evidence of our unity. I have come as a soldier in a great crusade of personal liberty as opposed to perpetual slavery.

"My faith in our ultimate victory is invincible and I bring to you tonight the unbreakable spirit of the free man's military code in support of our just cause. That code has come down to us from even before the days of knighthood and chivalry. It will stand the test of any ethics or philosophies the world has ever known. It embraces the things that are right and condemns the things that are wrong. Under its banner the free men of the world are united today.

"There can be no compromise. We shall win or we shall die, and to this end I pledge you the full resources of all the mighty power of my country and all the blood of my countrymen.

"Mr. Prime Minister, tonight will be an unforgettable memory for me. Your inspiring words and those of your compatriots will be emblazoned always in my memory as though they had been carved on stone or bronze.

"Under their inspiration I am taking the liberty of assuming the high honor of raising my glass in salute to your great country and its great leaders."

The cheers that followed were heard across the world.

* * * *

The following day MacArthur returned to Melbourne and to the task of organizing his Staff and formulating the duties of a Command that still was undefined and without directive. Certainly the picture of the advancing, conquering Jap forces was a menacing one. British Malaya, Singapore, and the Netherlands East Indies had already been completely overrun and vanquished. As early as January 23rd the Australian administrative center at Rabaul, on the great island of New Britain, had been cap-

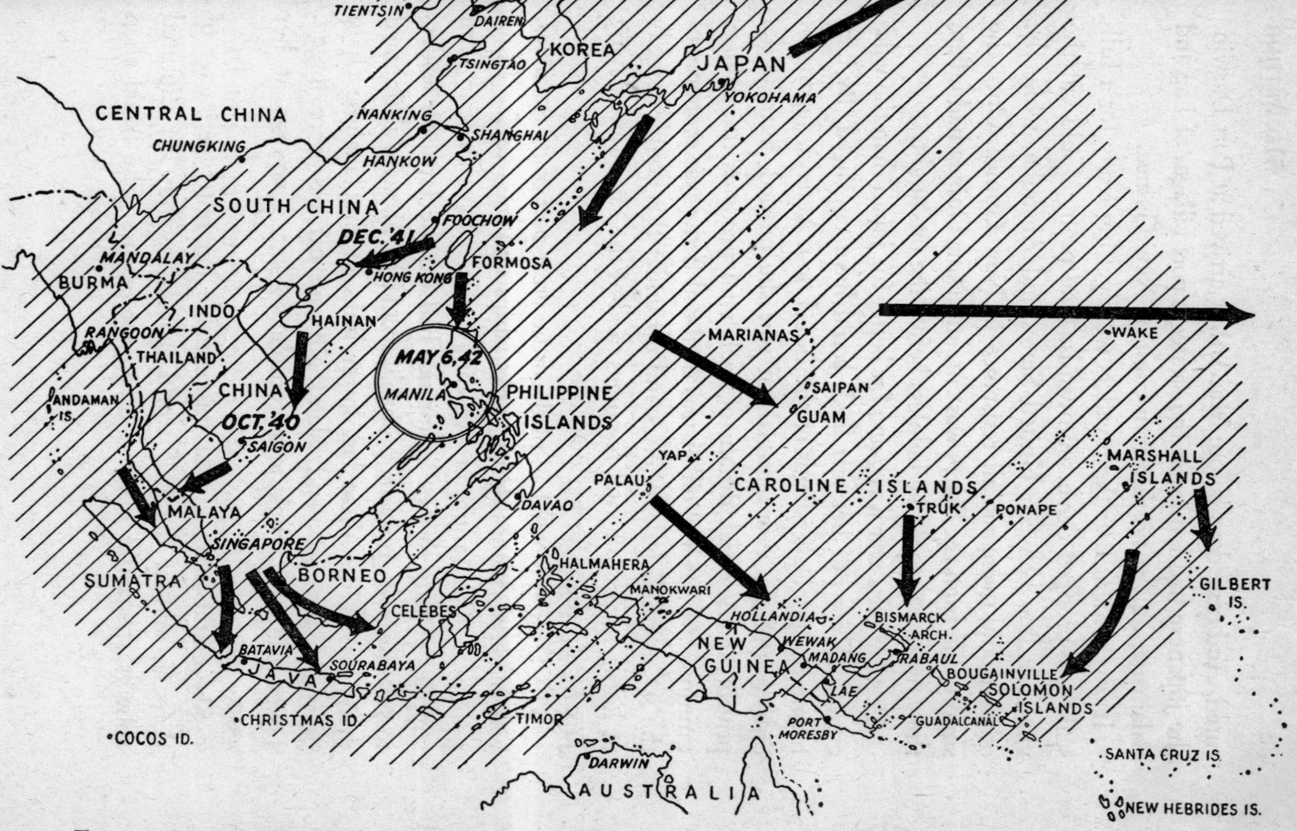

Extent of Japanese conquest and advance on March 17, 1942, when MacArthur arrived in Australia.

tured. And nine days before MacArthur arrived at Port Darwin, the Japanese had landed at the strategic port villages of Lae and Salamaua, on the northeastern coast of New Guinea.

It was evident that the invaders were getting ready for a full-scale two-pronged drive southwards. One prong would cut the vital life line between United States and Australia, while the other would overcome all resistance in New Guinea. Once the supply line from the States was cut, and New Guinea had fallen, then Australia would lie helpless before the onslaught.

Certainly the war was going far better for Japan than the wildest calculations of her war lords could have envisaged. By capturing the priceless islands of the N.E.I. and Malaya, Japan not only gained the raw materials of war she needed, but she deprived America and Britain of such vital needs as tin, rubber, quinine, and gas and oil. It was doubtful if the war economy of the Allies could indefinitely stand up under this double tragedy of losing its pool of vital resources, and at the same time having Japan gain them for her own use.

The United States had pledged the great part of its resources, war material, planes, guns, tanks, ships and men to the European war. The failure of Washington even to attempt to send supplies or help to the Philippines had led the Japanese leaders to surmise that Australia probably would be likewise abandoned to its fate. Once these last lower links in the Japanese chain of island fortresses and island airplane carriers were forged, Japan could sit back and consolidate her conquests at her ease.

She could make almost impregnable her outer perimeter of defense, and in the half world that lay within her captured spheres she could build a dominant empire. She could then challenge the arrogant white men when and where she chose to force the contest.

While America grew weaker through her lack of vital raw materials from Java and Malaya, Japan would constantly grow stronger. While America spent her men and ships and resources in the European war, the Pacific would slip from her grasp. The dream of ambitious Japanese leaders of nothing short of world conquest might well come true. The ring of island fortresses need only be extended a little further to the southward and even Australia would be theirs for the taking.

* * * *

All this was perfectly clear to MacArthur. Once again he knew he must fight with his back to the wall. Soon he must decide where and how he would fight to save this continent, and this western Pacific world.

There was talk everywhere of a so-called Brisbane Line of Defense. Everything north would be left open to invasion, but here in the southeastern tenth of the vast, discouraged continent, there was to be a last-ditch fight for the cities and the rich land around Brisbane, Sydney, Melbourne and Adelaide. This was the Living Heart of Australia, as against the great "Dead Heart" to the northwest.

Few of the Australian Imperial Forces, which included all of the experienced, well-trained and well-armed troops of the Commonwealth, had been brought home from distant Empire battlefronts. Brilliant and courageous as the outfits were, they by no means constituted a well-balanced, complete army. They were infantry divisions that had depended on outside British forces for their air support, for much of their transport, heavy artillery and special units. And save for a single Brigade of the 6th Division, they were not even in the country.

For her defense Australia had learned to depend upon the British Fleet. But at this time this great fleet was occupied in the Atlantic, Mediterranean and Indian oceans. It could not be spared for Australia.

Many units of Australian militia were being rapidly called up for service, but there were no arms at hand for them. Most of Australia's considerable war production had been sent overseas. The conscription law read that no Australian soldier could be sent outside the confines of his continent, unless he volunteered. By a special ruling the Australian mandated part of New Guinea, and as well, the part known as Papua, were lumped into the continental defense system, so that militiamen could be sent there.

As a matter of fact there were at this time some seven thousand Australian militiamen at the strategic key port of Moresby, in the southern tail of the great buzzard-shaped island of New Guinea. They were poorly equipped and only partially trained men. Already malaria was playing havoc with both the health and morale of these rugged men.

MacArthur at once sent two of his most competent men, Brigadier General Harold George of the Air Corps—who was soon to meet a tragic death—and his Engineer Brigadier General, Pat Casey, by plane to Moresby to make a survey of the situation. Meanwhile he slowly formulated his own conclusions. They would soon be fired and tempered in the furnace of his resolve—and from this final steel decision nothing would ever deflect him.

"We'll make the fight for Australia up in New Guinea," he

finally said to Sutherland and Marshall. He was to say it over and over again. He was to gain faith and courage from it. He would not accept the sure defeat of defense. He would go out and meet the enemy on battlefields of his, and not the enemy's choosing.

It became the slogan of his staff—"We'll make the fight for Australia up in New Guinea." It made little difference to him what his ultimate directives from Washington might be. He would not sit back and be destroyed by permitting the enemy to come to him. He would choose the time and place.

He had few arms, few planes, few troops—but he had the will to win. He had made it come alive, true and unconquerable, that black night in the corridor of his Melbourne car. He had recaptured the faith then; now he had chosen his battlefield.

But he was still a man without a command, without orders, without a directive. It was embarrassing, to say the least. He could not make his final arrangements with the Australians, or the Dutch, or even with the United States Forces that were here. He wired Washington over and over to have such vital matters as the limits of his theater cleared up. Finally on April 18th, after he had been in the country a full month plus a day, his directive arrived.

In place of New Zealand, New Caledonia, and the eastern portions of the Solomon Islands being included in his theater, he was to be limited on the east to the 160th meridian and on the other side to west of the 105th meridian. Wavell's command, the old ABDA area, which would have been the logical assignment, now had its eastern and western thirds shorn away and MacArthur was left only the central sector. Most of the parts outside of Australia were in enemy possession.

But he now had his orders, and he would defend Australia—and defend it in the precipitous jungle reaches of the Owen Stanley range in New Guinea. To fail in this would mean that the Japanese could push on southward and then infiltrate in force into the rich Australian coastal cities when and how they wished.

He would defend Australia to the last bit of his strength—but he would defend it by going north to meet the enemy. "We'll make the fight for Australia up in New Guinea," he grimly repeated.

On that he would not give an inch. He would fight—and he had chosen where and how.

But he had at best so little to do the job with.

* * * *

Casey and George flew back from Moresby with a report that was anything but encouraging. Moresby, by far the most important harbor on the southwest shore of the tail of Guinea, was defended by two brigades of Australian militia. The men were discouraged, half-sick and half-armed. They were largely concerned with getting home, and then fighting the invaders in their own back yards.

On the outskirts of the tropical port the observers found at "Seven Mile" a dinky airfield with one strip that was deficient in drainage and was badly surfaced. A single Australian Engineer company was operating a nearby rock quarry with native labor. It was all make-shift, and inadequate. Beside this "Seven Mile" field there was one small commercial airdrome at Kila, but not even a fighter could have landed on it. Fighters, however, could land and take off from "Seven Mile."

From Moresby a trail or track zigzagged across the misty high passes of the Owen Stanley mountains that stretched like the dorsal vertebrae of some prehistoric animal down the middle of this interminable jungle island. It was clear to MacArthur that if he wanted to hold strategic New Guinea he must immediately build a strong air and sea base here at Moresby; and then grab and hold certain key points at the very lowest point of the tail, and along the northeastern shore line.

For a day or two he toyed with the idea of having Casey build a road over the mountains, through Kokoda Pass and then on down to the little port of Buna on the eastern coast. But it was obvious that such inadequate engineering equipment and forces as Casey had should be thrown into the vital and immediate task of building airfields. In this phase of the war, planes and ships were the most important weapons. Planes needed airfields, and ships needed harbors. Each was dependent on the other. Ships could not operate unless the skies were free of enemy bombers. That required air bases; and those, in turn, were useless unless ground troops held them, and men, supplies, food, oil and spare parts could safely be brought in by boat. In the new warfare, the sea was sister to the skies, and both were based on the ground.

MacArthur ordered his Chief Engineer to push through adequate air facilities here at Moresby as fast as he possibly could. With the speed, energy and improvising genius that are peculiar to American engineers, the work was immediately started. The 96th colored U. S. Engineer Battalion, with its scanty equipment, was hustled by boat to Moresby. They were the first American ground forces actually to land in this historic battleground. They were materially to help save Guinea and Australia and the Western Pacific.

* * * *

While Casey was pushing through his first Guinea air strips, and MacArthur was struggling to whip together a Staff, organize his tiny forces, and then begin begging for men and weapons and supplies, there were great and important things happening on the sea in this Jap-infested part of the world. Some of those things had occurred while MacArthur was still fighting the good fight in Bataan.

For instance, on February 19th and 20th of 1942, planes from a single U. S. carrier, operating with four cruisers and ten destroyers, tangled with a great force of Japanese bombers out from Rabaul. Butch O'Hare alone shot down five bombers, and of the twenty enemy planes only one got away. It was the first serious set-back the Japanese had received in this part of the world. Among other things it proved that even land-based bombers attacking a Navy Task Force that had its own carriers must be accompanied by a fighter escort.

Then on March 10th, the exact day that MacArthur left the grim ruins of Corregidor, an American Task Force of two carriers, eight cruisers and fourteen destroyers, moved into the upper Coral Sea. Undiscovered, they shot their dive bombers and torpedo-carrying planes to Moresby, then through the mists and thunderheads of the Owen Stanley range and over the 12,000-foot peaks, and with the sun to their back hit a Japanese armada lying peacefully at anchor at Lae-Salamaua. When the duck shooting was over the carrier-based dive bombers had sunk five Japanese transports, two heavy cruisers, one light cruiser, three destroyers, one minelayer and one gunboat, and had damaged another gunboat and a seaplane tender. Our total loss was one scout plane that had been shot down in the jungle over Lae by AA fire. Because they had come swinging in from the west over the Owen Stanley range, the Nips were certain the planes were land-based bombers from northern Australia. They never suspected that they had come from Navy carriers.

By the time MacArthur had set up his Headquarters in Melbourne, bad news was beginning to come in from the Philippines. Food was running low, morale was dropping. MacArthur was distraught. The question of a possible surrender was raised from Washington. What were MacArthur's views on the subject? He replied that he was utterly opposed to surrender and asked that he should be permitted to return at once to the Philippines and personally attempt a break through. He felt sure that he could fly back safely.

During moments of discouragement, long before he had been ordered by the President to Australia, he had worked out in detail the possibility of a last desperate venture to break his way out from the trap of Bataan. By a sudden enveloping movement on the right and then a change of direction to the left, with a simultaneous drive from the left itself, he would attempt to overwhelm the enemy's base at Olongapo Base on Subic Bay, seize his transports and attempt to reach Mindanao by sea and join General Sharp. Other elements would rapidly disintegrate into the Zambales Mountains of Luzon for guerrilla warfare.

Washington liked the plan but felt he should not return to put it into effect.

There was nothing that MacArthur could do now.

Bataan surrendered within the week. To MacArthur it was a taste like unto death. But he maintained then, and has maintained ever since, a complete reserve with reference to it. His only statement was as touching as it was brief:

"The Bataan Force went out as it would have wished, fighting to the end its flickering forlorn hope. No army has ever done so much with so little, and nothing became it more than its last hour of trial and agony. To the weeping mothers of its dead, I can only say that the sacrifice and halo of Jesus of Nazareth has descended upon their Sons, and that God will take them unto Himself."

* * * *

Now came the Coral Sea fight that stretched from May 4th to the 8th. It was the first great naval battle in history where no surface ship even saw an enemy ship, and no ship's horizontal gun was fired. It was fought in the air between carrier-based planes—a deadly battle of the skies. The Japanese were repulsed and their plan to land troops by sea at Port Moresby was frustrated.

It was a victory that eased a little of the heartache that was saddening MacArthur and those about him. On May 7th word came that Corregidor had fallen. It was a crushing blow to MacArthur. On a pad he wrote out by pencil a single paragraph:

"Corregidor needs no comment from me. It has sounded its own story at the mouth of its guns. It has scrolled its own epitaph on enemy tablets. But through the bloody haze of its last reverberating shot, I shall always see a vision of grim, gaunt, ghostly men, still unafraid."

It was a soldier's last tribute to his comrades.

CHAPTER SIX

ON July 20, 1942, MacArthur moved his Headquarters from Melbourne to Brisbane, Queensland. He was now 1,200 miles nearer his selected battlefield, New Guinea. Later he would move his advanced echelon into a rambling old bungalow in colorful, hot and frightened Port Moresby. He would live here during most of the big operations that were to follow.

A portion of his time he still was required to spend in his base Headquarters in Queensland. It was essential for him to keep in constant touch with the Australian government officials and with the army leaders. This could only be done in Australia itself.

A modern hotel had been requisitioned. In it were lodged the senior officers of his Headquarters staff. A double suite of rooms with simple housekeeping facilities, was reserved for the General and his family. Here the capable and loyal Jean MacArthur, little Arthur and Ah Chuh, the faithful old Chinese servant, were installed.

He realized fully the enormity of the task ahead and the paucity of resources he had to work with. There was no moment to lose, and no second to waste. He must conserve the last ounce of his energy and time. He must let nothing interfere with the work at hand. There was much hard thinking to be done, many grave problems to challenge his resourcefulness.

The military demands would be so heavy that he would have to forego all social activities. Of necessity the life of this little family was to be one of simple dignity, almost monastic in its call of duty. Two or three playmates were found for the little boy.

Now and again some old friend of the army or an army nurse from the Philippines, made brief afternoon calls on Mrs. MacArthur. Her work was here with her husband. Her job was to keep him well and fit, and to give him the sanctuary of a quiet, smooth-running home—even though it had to be in a busy hotel. His meals were of the simplest—his wife herself preparing most of them. He drank little or nothing, and his only indulgence was a few pipefuls of tobacco each day, and a single after-dinner cigar.

Altogether it was a Spartan life the General and his little family led. He could work out his problems and make his final decisions in peace and quiet. His great military experience, his deep thinking and study combined to give his work the sure touch. He could afford to make no mistakes. The issues involved were too important, and those who would humiliate and destroy him too powerful to be given even half a chance.

* * * *

MacArthur had only the barest shoestring to fight with. On April 6th the 41st U. S. Infantry Division arrived in Adelaide, and on May 14th the 32nd U. S. Division landed. Brigades of the three veteran Australian divisions from the Middle East were beginning to come home—but compared to the forces of the enemy it was still only a shoestring force. It was unbalanced at best, and short of service troops, water transport and air units.

The trickle of supplies from America was now a little wider, but the Southwest Pacific was still less than a 10 percent war—and actually the supplies sent to MacArthur were no more than 10 percent of those sent to North Africa alone. It was to remain that for the next two years of peril and hardship. Never was this great and vital Southwest Pacific theater to receive as much as 10 percent of America's total war effort.

Briefly stated, MacArthur's fundamental problem was to stop the advance of the Japanese that threatened New Guinea, gather such forces as he could and then strike back. To defend Australia successfully he must fight the attackers in Guinea.

He already had one important toehold—Port Moresby—midway up on the southern shore of the tail of this vast weird-shaped island. It is a wild forbidding land, a land where thousands of square miles have never felt the tread of white men; an ominous land of jungle and mountains, rain forests and fever swamps.

To reach the eastern shore of the Guinea tail Allied troops and supplies would have to move across the high passes of the great Owen Stanley mountains that swung down through the center of the peninsula like a gigantic spinal column.

The Japanese were already securely planted on the eastern Guinea shore at both Lae and Salamaua. The mountains apparently protected Moresby from any Japanese attack from there. Crossing the high range was a mud track that passed over the hump leading by the native village of Kokoda—which gave its name to this trail.

But this high mountain range apparently was not only a barrier against Japanese attack from the east Guinea coast, but as well a barrier to Allied advance. MacArthur figured that if he could grab the tiny native village of Milne Bay, at the extreme southwestern tip of the Guinea tail, quickly build air strips and develop a port there, he could then move by sea and air up the rugged eastern shoreline—and thus obviate the need of going directly over the great Owen Stanley range to join battle with the Japanese.

By late July, he had built airfields and bomber strips at Moresby, and he could now move stealthily some 250 miles on southeast, down the west Guinea coast to Milne Bay. From here he anticipated that he could make an end run, a couple of hundred miles on up the east Guinea coast to the string of tiny native villages called Buna, Sananda and Gona. Once these were in his hands, he could build advance airfields, bring in his fighters and eventually his bombers, secure air control—and the lower Papuan quarter of New Guinea would be his.

But he had neither the men nor the equipment, neither the ships nor the amphibious vessels to do the job. He was driving the few people and machines he had as hard as they could be driven. He had said in his brief talk on his arrival at Melbourne, "No General can make something out of nothing." He still had practically nothing—save will and courage, and an infinite capacity to work. Even time was against him.

On July 22nd black news came to his Headquarters: Buna and Gona had that day been occupied by the Japanese. MacArthur's tiny air force had failed to stop the Japanese convoy. The optimistic plan he had made to push his way up the eastern coast of Guinea had disappeared in the mists and rain of the jungle shore. But the key to New Guinea was still Milne Bay—and the key was his.

He ordered his engineers to redouble their efforts at Milne Bay. They begged, borrowed and stole a forlorn batch of equipment and transport; on their overcrowded ships they carried steel landing mats for the air strips. It was a rag, tag and bobtail outfit, but if MacArthur wanted them to build him an airstrip in hell, they'd do it. This mosquito-buzzing, rain-soaked green jungle wasn't very far removed from that slightly over-advertised locality at best.

Suddenly a fresh and dangerous threat faced MacArthur's

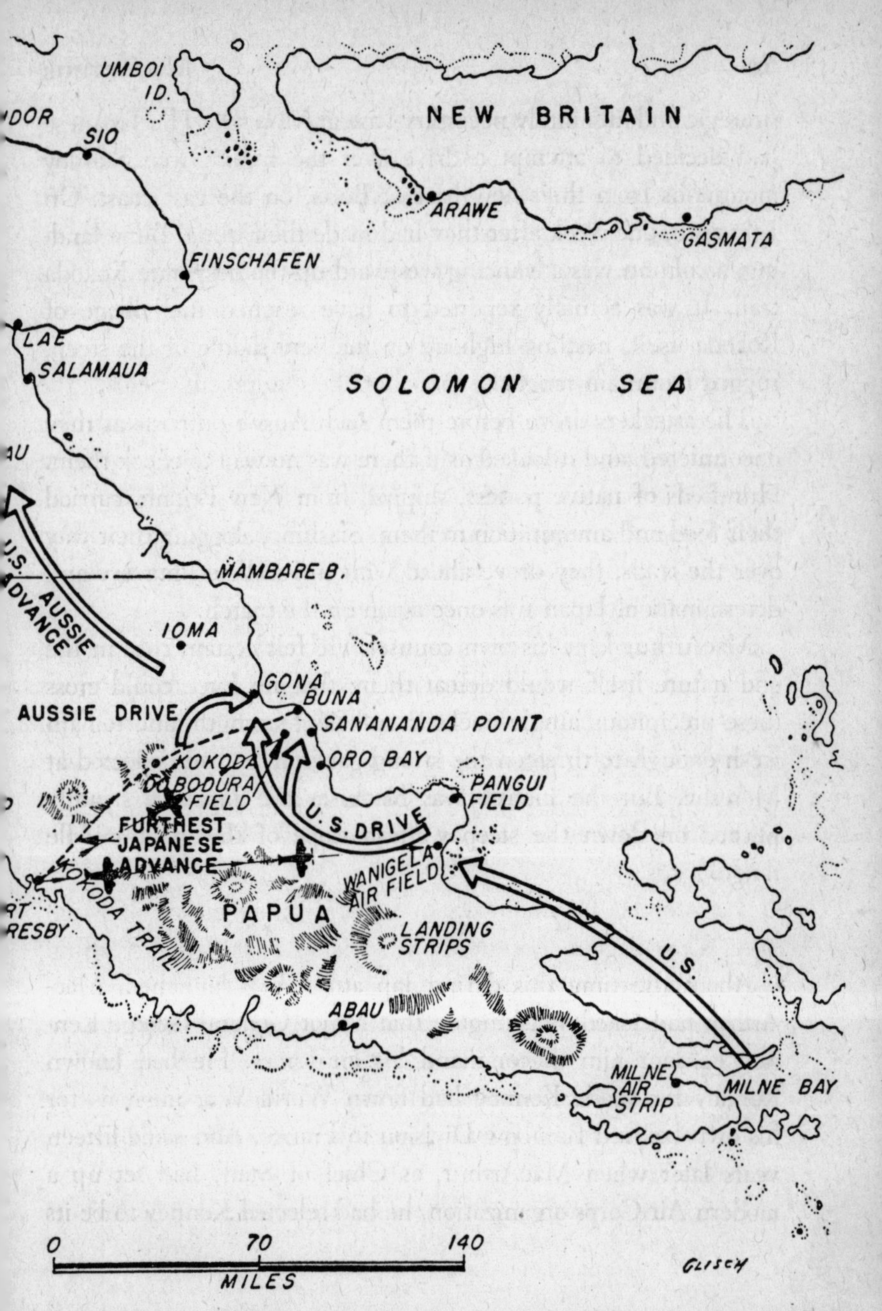

six deadly months Yanks and Aussies fought against heavy Japanese odds to apture this southern tip of New Guinea and give MacArthur the offensive.

strategic and absolutely necessary base at Moresby. The Japanese had decided to attempt a drive over the high Owen Stanley mountains from their new base at Buna, on the east coast. On July 29th, one week after they had made their initial Buna landing, a column was advancing westward up the desperate Kokoda trail. It was actually reported to have reached the village of Kokoda itself, nestling high up on the very saddle of the steep, rugged mountain range.

The attackers drove before them such Aussie outposts as they encountered, and it looked as if there was no way to check them. Hundreds of native porters, shipped from New Britain, carried their food and ammunition to them. Slashing, slogging their way over the trails, they drove ahead with unparalleled bravery and determination. Japan was once again on the march.

MacArthur kept his own counsel. He felt certain that in the end nature itself would defeat them; that no force could cross these precipitous jungle tracks in sufficient strength, and remain fresh enough to threaten the strong garrison he had collected at Moresby. But the picture was black, as the Japanese steadily pushed on down the steep western slope of the great middle range.

* * * *

About the time this daring Jap attack was launched, MacArthur had asked Washington that Major General George Kenney be sent him to command his air forces. He had known Kenney for years. Kenney had flown World War missions for his own beloved Rainbow Division in France. And some fifteen years later when MacArthur, as Chief of Staff, had set up a modern Air Corps organization, he had selected Kenney to be its operations officer. The two men understood each other thoroughly. MacArthur regarded Kenney as "the finest air commander he had ever known." And Kenney had said of his Chief, "He knows more about the strategic handling of air forces and has more imagination in their use than any commander in the world."

"The air force here needs revamping and tightening up, George," MacArthur explained to Kenney when he arrived. Tireless Kenney shook it up from top to bottom, and swiftly it became MacArthur's good right arm—his striking fist. This Fifth Air Force eventually was to be the terror of the skies, spreading death, destruction and fear. But long and discouraging months would pass before the needed planes and men would be sent to the Pacific.

In late July, 1942, MacArthur had a grand total of 466 planes in his American Air Force. They were scattered over dozens of airfields. Not one in five was mechanically ready to fly. Of sixty-seven Fortresses exactly six were in full commission. It is an accepted fact that it is usually impossible to maintain in combat flight at any time, more than forty percent of any total strength. The flying efficiency of the air force Kenney took over was considerably lower than that classic figure.

The garrisoning of Milne Bay was now rapidly progressing. With unerring judgment MacArthur had anticipated a Japanese attack in force on this strategic finger tip, and had prepared as best he could. He had sent down the major part of two Australian infantry brigades, and their commander had posted them to defend the priceless fields that were being rushed to completion.

On the night of August 25th the Japanese landed. The fighting that followed was bloody and decisive. Japanese destroyers shelled at night. Their tanks moved forward, but bogged down in the muddy trails. Their foot soldiers pushed on, advancing through the deadly melee, on up through the jungle and swamp towards the airfields.

At Strip No. 3 a heterogeneous mass of defenders lay hidden in the woods at the edge of the narrow mile-long air strip that lay between them and the advancing Japanese. It gave them an effective clear field of fire against the attackers.

At one end of the thinly held defensive line was part of an Australian battalion. At the other end was a platoon of a U. S. anti-aircraft unit. In the middle were two companies of the 46th U. S. Engineers, with a 50-caliber machine gun mounted on a truck.

A single Japanese stepped out of the woods on to the edge of the center of the air strip. A concealed Yank Engineer sergeant took a dead aim with his 50-caliber gun. He squeezed the trigger—and nothing happened. He had forgotten to unbolt the firing pin.

Before he could get his heavy machine gun working the Jap scout stepped back into the woods. Apparently he concluded there were no Yanks or Aussies about. The Japs now broke out of the woods in mass, moving straight across the field. Then the Yanks and Aussies let go. It was murder in the first degree. When the battle was over there were 257 dead Japs left behind to be buried by the Engineers. The wounded had been carried off.

The Aussie reserves now drove in, pushed back the Japanese columns—and all the time Yank and Aussie bombers and strafers got in their deadly work. In the end such Japanese as were not killed were forced to their boats—and the Battle of Milne Bay was history.

MacArthur had completely fooled the enemy, for instead of finding an inadequate outpost, the Nip found himself hopelessly outnumbered and outclassed. The defeat was complete. It was the decisive factor in this phase of the desperate Guinea campaign.

* * * *

In the meantime, a couple of hundred miles on to the northward the weird drama of the Kokoda trail was unfolding itself in the dank rain forests and slippery western slopes of the Owen Stanley range. The Japanese had now reached a point in the mountain trail less than thirty miles from Moresby. They had little further to go—a bare thirty miles. They had courage and fanatical devotion—but they were utterly exhausted. They just couldn't make it.

Yet they were only a day or two away from their prize. A single day's march and they could have dominated the airfields on the outskirts of Moresby. Once the Japanese could get these fields, they could land their fighters and bombers here, drive out the defenders, clean up lower New Guinea—and start the invasion of northeastern Australia.

MacArthur was in supreme command, but his Diggers were directly under Lt. General Rowell, an able leader who had been tested in the crucible of Greece and the Middle East. MacArthur instructed him to check and then roll back the Japanese columns, regardless of the cost. Rowell had at hand elements of the battle-proven 7th Division, A.I.F.—under the immediate command of Major General Vasey. When the moment came to make the countercharge he threw in the brilliant Brigadier Eather and the 25th Brigade. Eather smashed at the Japanese spearhead, enveloped it, and drove it into the steep gorges of the vast mountain wilderness.

The series of relentless up-hill drives on up the Kokoda trail that followed wrote a deathless chapter in the history of both Australian and Allied arms.

The overall planning had been done by MacArthur, but the hard fighting in this initial part of this bitter campaign—that later was to end in the death swamps of Buna—was done by brave "dinkum" Aussies.

As MacArthur had calculated, the Japanese columns were now completely exhausted. Their carriers deserted them, our air force relentlessly pounded them, and tall, gaunt Aussies struck back at them night and day. They did not wait to make a last stand, but in the end turned back towards Buna, denying mile by mile the long ghostly trail over the high ridges and through the mists and mysteries of the passes.

For the first time MacArthur was no longer threatened. For the moment he was the master of the land and the gray skies above these deadly purple mountains of the Owen Stanley range. Now was the time for him to hit hard—to close in and slug it out, with Buna as the prize.

As it would be throughout all the Guinea campaigns that were to follow, the most difficult problem to solve was communication and supply. MacArthur, somehow or other, had to find a way to get his troops, guns and equipment over this high Owen Stanley range, and plant them in the plain around Buna, on the eastern side of the mountains.

Already he had columns of his jungle-wise Aussies slogging back over the Kokoda trail, driving the Japanese rear guard before them. They were now marching down the trail on the eastern slopes, which led to the plains of Buna, Sanananda and Gona on the north. Quickly he had Kenney fly in a company of the 126th U. S. Infantry. The rest of the regiment was sent by boat to Moresby. In the meantime the entire 128th Infantry was flown in to Moresby from the mainland.

But this would only be a drop in the bucket. MacArthur must find a way to bring in large quantities of American troops and supplies from the southwest, planting them here on the Buna plains, for later use as the lower jaw of the giant nutcracker, that would close in on the Japanese in Buna, Gona and Sananda area.

The Aussies coming down the Kokoda trail would be the upper jaw of the cracker.

Now if airfields could be secured near Buna, MacArthur might have Kenney fly in doughboys and supplies, and here in the rear and on the left flank of the Japanese he might build up sufficient forces to launch a real attack against the Buna area.

Native laborers would be needed to hack out temporary strips in the fields of waving Kunai grass. On these simple strips slow-landing transport planes could come down with men, machines and supplies. And soon a field tough and long enough for fighters could be built. Eventually even bombers could be set down.

From a spot on the west coast below Moresby, a lean, experienced Norwegian-born, St. Louis-trained engineer and jungle pathfinder—one Colonel Jack Sverdrup—was sent out to cross the mountains on foot, cut out temporary strips, and finally help build a great air base right under the nose of the enemy close by Buna, at a spot called Dobadura. Sverdrup gathered a force of 297 natives, armed with shovels, axes and machetes, and in sixteen days these tireless black boys walked one hundred seventy miles of mountain trail, hacked out four temporary strips, with Wanigela the final one—and then were ready for the big job at Dobadura.

Wanigela strip was prospected by landing a light plane in the high Kunai grass. Natives cut a strip, and Kenney flew in 1,000 Aussies.

Dobadura came next. It was a scant ten miles below and to the west of the Japanese stronghold at Buna. Here were found narrow corridors of tall Kunai grass, stretching between parallel bands of jungle. Each grass corridor was a potential landing strip. There was nothing between the Japanese at Buna and Sverdrup's men but this almost impenetrable jungle. But before the Japanese were aware of what was going on a temporary strip was hacked out of the tough Kunai grass. Then the transports landed with protecting troops. Then more came, with engineers, knocked-down bulldozers, and scrapers. For the first time in all history grunting road-making machines were given wings.

Soon fighters were landing and taking off. That was a great day for MacArthur. These fighters could now drive off the enemy dive bombers from up the coast, while the field was being enlarged and straightened for the heavy bombers. It would be the springboard for further advances—for pushing forward his deadly Bomber Line. (Turn back to map on page 93.)

To MacArthur's alert, calculating eye this field at Dobadura was the key to the whole Buna campaign that was now shaping up. The Japanese field at Buna, only ten miles away, was waterlogged and unserviceable. The field here at Dobadura was perfectly drained and usable in all kinds of weather.

It was a real air base, close up to the enemy lines, and on his flank and rear. With it in working order, MacArthur was now ready to make his great move—and one that would send chills up and down the spines of even the tough Japanese.

Suddenly out of the misty skies lumbering old transport planes began to land—and out from their broad bellies jumped Yank doughboys, motors, equipment, ammunition, food and even drums of gas. In a matter of a few days Kenney flew in from northern Australia the entire 128th Infantry—more than 3,000 men. It was as far as from Miami to Chicago. Then he flew in a complete field hospital, operating tables, doctors and all. In the single month of December he evacuated by air 7,200 wounded and sick men and replaced them with fresh troops that were desperately needed.

MacArthur ordered him to fly in a battery of 105-mm. howitzers, complete with half-tracks, ammunition and men. That almost stumped Kenney—but only for a moment. He set down a B-17 E on the field in Brisbane, and hurriedly built a temporary floor in the right bomb bay. Then he took the 4,325-pound howitzer apart and fitted it in the good old Fort as neatly as a dentist puts an inlay in a cavity. Next he took down the prime-mover, and tucked its 1,600 pounds of parts wherever he could find room. In the odds and ends of space that still remained he jammed in 1,250 pounds of shells, 200 pounds of kit, 800 pounds of equipment; and then he wedged in the eight gunners and their gear, another matter of 2,000 pounds. Altogether that one air-borne gun outfit totalled 10,175 pounds. There wasn't an empty pocket left big enough to have held a female mosquito.

Two days later several thousand misguided patriots from Nippon had the shock of their lives when 105-millimeter shells began lobbing into their nests and gun emplacements from their rear, deep in the jungle. Many of them went to their honored ancestors before they figured out how that gun ever got there.

* * * *

MacArthur, and his air arm, had lifted war to new dimensions. At Crete, the spring before this, the Germans had won unbelievable victories with transport planes and gliders—but they had had the whole great Luftwaffe to draw from and their operations were unopposed by the RAF. MacArthur and Kenney had only their shoestring force. In the encircled Mediterranean distances were small, and there were always unlimited stocks of Nazi planes, men and supplies. Here at the end of the world MacArthur and his air chief worked with what was at hand, improvising, letting Yankee ingenuity and resourcefulness serve their many needs.

It was a war of great distances and incredible hardships. Never had ground troops been called upon to fight such a fanatical enemy in such deadly jungle and mud and endless danger. Yet they never gave up.

MacArthur at last was ready to close in his great envelopment movement on the three native villages. On the north, or left flank, the rugged Australians under Lt. General Herring were pushing towards the coastal towns of Sananda and Gona. On the right flank, pointing north and east towards Buna, were the Yankees of the 32nd Division under Lt. General Bob Eichelberger, I Corps Commander. Between the two forces lay the impassable swamp delta of a wide tropical river. This swamp split the two Allied groups squarely in the middle.

Both Allied forces were confronted by a series of strongly developed Japanese defensive positions, bunker-type machine

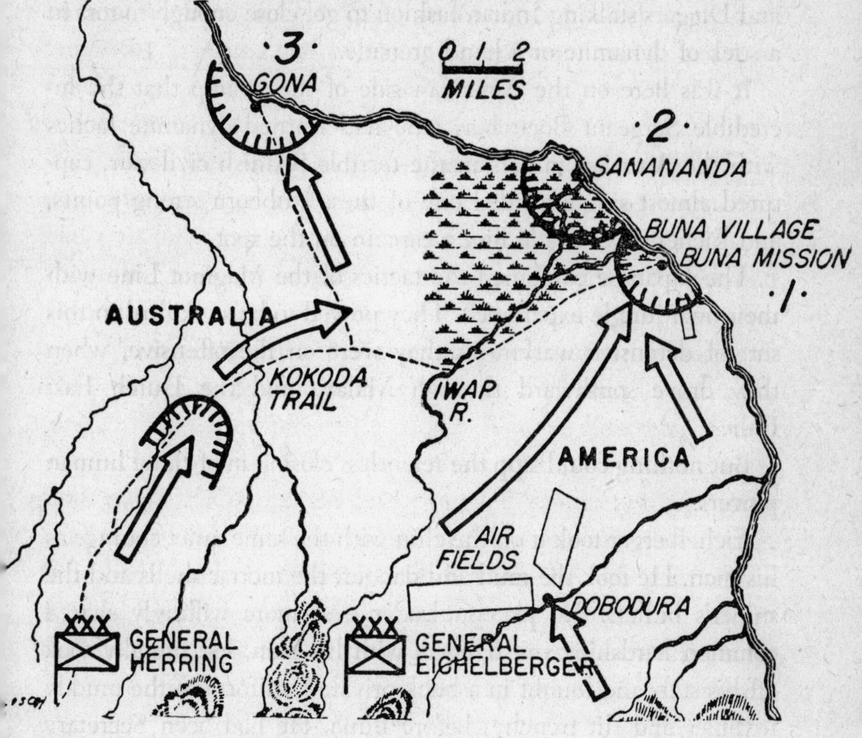

Where Yanks and Aussies fought side by side, yet separated by swamps and ollen tropical rivers in the most desperate campaign of the whole Guinea war.

gun nests and pill boxes—which from now on were to be the hallmark of Japanese defenses in the Guinea theater. They were underground, heavily shored with tree trunks, with narrow firing slits that resembled small window sashes. They were completely camouflaged, and melted unsuspectingly into the surrounding bush. Many of them had to be shot out of existence by point-blank artillery fire. Others had to be taken by intrepid doughboys and Diggers stalking Indian fashion to get close enough to toss in a stick of dynamite or a hand grenade.

It was here on the American side of the swamp that the incredible Sergeant Boettcher, who had learned dynamite tactics with the Asturian miners in the terrible Spanish civil war, captured almost single-handed one of these stubborn strong points, and Eichelberger made him a captain on the spot.

The Japanese combined the tactics of the Maginot Line with their own jungle experience. They proved to be as skillful in this sort of defensive warfare as they were on the offensive, when they drove southward through Malaya and the Dutch East Indies.

But nothing could stop the relentless closing-in of those human pincers.

Eichelberger took it on the chin with the same quiet courage as his men. He took the mud and danger, the mortar shells and the sniper's bullets. No platoon leader ever more willingly shared common hardships and dangers with his men. He literally took off his stars and fought in a buck private's uniform in the muddy foxholes and slit trenches before Buna. He had been Secretary of the General Staff when MacArthur was head of the Army. And when night closed in on the weird silences of the swamps and rain forests of the Buna plains, this tall, fearless soldier could hear the echoes of MacArthur's vibrant voice as he gave him his final orders: "Bob, get me Buna! Don't come back alive without it!" And Bob Eichelberger didn't.

Notch by notch, step by step, the pincers closed in on the doomed Japanese positions. Aussie tanks finally broke into the Buna airfield, while the Yanks moved into Buna Village. On December 9th, five days before this, the Diggers had overrun the

Gona area. On January 2nd, Buna Government Station was captured. And three weeks later Sananända was overrun. The wearisome, desperate Buna campaign was over.

It was the end to the Japanese advance in New Guinea. The threat to Australia was no more. MacArthur could now take the offensive. He would now choose his own time and place to attack. His one barometer was the meager forces and equipment that were being doled out to him.

But he was now on the move. Step by step he would climb up the long, hard ladder that led to the north.

Somehow or other his shoestring force would become an army on the march. It was still starved and neglected. But it was headed in the right direction.

CHAPTER SEVEN

THE PATTERN OF THE FIRST GENERAL OFFENSIVE IN THE South-west Pacific area began to take shape early in 1943. Briefly, it was a great double envelopment with the two strong arms moving north, operating some six hundred miles from one another.

MacArthur's strategy was to push one arm of the giant nut-cracker up through the Solomons on the right, and the other up the New Guinea coast on the left; then to close in on the long, narrow island of New Britain and pinch off the whole of the Solomon Sea. This would be Bear Hug Number One.

The original line of demarcation between Halsey in the Southern Pacific and MacArthur's theater had been the 160th degree of longitude, but in order to include all of Guadalcanal in Halsey's territory, this line had been moved one degree to the West. When Guadalcanal fell, Halsey's remaining objectives in the Solomons and Bismarcks lay in MacArthur's theater. The joint Chiefs of Staff placed Halsey under MacArthur's strategic command and his forces thus became MacArthur's right wing.

Had either of the two been lesser men it might have been an unhappy situation, but they were kindred fighting spirits and their cooperation became a model for the services. Halsey remembered the magnificent help MacArthur had given him in neutralizing the enemy's air force in Rabaul at the expense of his own operations during the hour of danger at Guadalcanal, and he promptly announced that he was proud to serve under MacArthur.

From the standpoint of means at his disposal MacArthur's decision to take the offensive was bold, almost rash, thinking. He was short of everything—men, planes, guns, ships, small boats and amphibious equipment. He was hampered and hamstrung in a score of ways. The mention of his name as a possible Republican candidate continued to echo up and down Pennsylvania Avenue, from the White House to the Capitol. Starting as a whisper it had become almost a roar.

As far back as October, 1942, MacArthur took the bull by the horns and issued a formal statement that should have satisfied those who considered him a threat in a political way. At that time he said: "I have no political ambitions whatsoever. Any suggestion to the contrary must be regarded as merely amiable gestures of goodwill dictated by friendship. I started as a soldier and I shall finish as one. The only hope and ambition I have in the world is for victory for our cause in the war. If I survive the campaign, I shall return to that retirement from which this great struggle called me."

But even this did not seem to satisfy. MacArthur was able to stand what was said in detraction of him personally, but he resented to the bottom of his being the handicaps and penalties that his theater suffered. The inadequate forces and equipment that were being sent him were excused by such broad half-truths as "first things must come first." The principle that the mass of everything must go to Europe, while the Western Pacific would have to stand or fall on what was left over, was laid down as immutable and beyond argument.

Jealous men could ease their conscience by the claim of formal pledges made to our Allies—and often, without legal authority. MacArthur's views were dismissed as a special bad case of "Localitis." Every locality and war theater was shouting for more and more men, planes and equipment. MacArthur was just one of them, Washington officials glibly explained.

But the net result of all this was that MacArthur was compelled to enter his first real offensive campaign with a force so inadequate that it would have been a gruesome joke had it not been beset by constant threat of disaster. He had started with a shoestring force, and all through this moving year of 1943 it was to remain a shoestring force.

Yet this very inadequacy had a strange result, for out of it came a new technique, a completely new application of the solid old principles of war. Air power would have to be fitted into amphibious action; surprise would have to offset great mass; every weapon and service must be used to its maximum; weakness of one would have to be covered by the strength of the other.

Always he would have to do much with little. He would have to exploit weather, terrain, secret intelligence information, and a deep knowledge of the character of his foe.

He did not have the men and matériel, the ships and equipment, to indulge in any costly frontal attacks—even had he so desired. He had to husband his stinted forces, and by perfect coordination, balance and a nicety of timing, practice to the limit of his skill the art of war. He had to select with utmost care and daring his definite objectives. *He could not afford to make mistakes.*

He could not partake of great retreats—"strategic withdrawals" is the proper Hollywood term for such disasters. He had no reserves to fall back on.

And even if he had had these luxuries of war he had at home no great voices to explain away his mistakes, and in beautiful phrases to deceive the humble, patriotic people of the world whose sons were being used up in campaigns badly conceived, badly led—but brilliantly advertised. Wars, like third-rate surgeons, bury their mistakes.

War had long been a horrible business to MacArthur. He had seen much of it in the first World War. The battle ribbons he had won were pinned straight into his heart. Early in the Buna campaign he said to one of his general officers: "Let us spill no unnecessary blood. I have seen too many men slaughtered in past wars through error and bad judgment."

And never was an American boy or a brave Aussie to die unnecessarily.

MacArthur's plan for his return to the Philippines was to advance by the establishment of a series of air and naval bases along the land mass of the impenetrable jungle of New Guinea. This concept called for the full use of balanced air, land and sea forces. But since his sea forces were entirely inadequate, he proposed to advance anyway, by covering his water movements by land-based fighters and bombers.

But before he could move north from Buna and Dobadura, on up to Lae and Salamaua and beyond, it was essential to secure safe passage through the Vitiaz Straits. To do this, a powerful Japanese air force based on the great Rabaul bastion had to be neutralized.

The enemy that MacArthur and Halsey faced was strongly entrenched in New Guinea, the Bismarcks, Admiralties and Solomons south to Guadalcanal. At the very eastern tip of New Britain the Japanese had built in Rabaul a vast naval base and four great airfields, heavily defended by fighter and anti-aircraft guns. Other airfields were scattered about New Britain, and on this island alone were not less than seventy thousand experienced Japanese troops.

The Japanese position was like a huge horseshoe. New Britain Island was the toe of the horseshoe; the Solomon Archipelago was one shaft; the southwestern peninsula of New Guinea, six hundred miles to the westward, was the other shaft. In the empty center lay the Solomon Sea. This horseshoe the enemy had nailed down with air and navy bases.

Guarding the Vitiaz Straits on the west were the strong bases of Lae, Salamaua, Finschhafen, and Saidor. Across the straits on Western New Britain were Gloucester, Arawe and Gasmata. Opposing Halsey's advance on the right were New Georgia, Munda, Vella Lavella, Buin-Faisi, Bougainville, Buka—and strongest of all, Rabaul.

As far back as August 6th, the day before the Marines had landed on Guadalcanal, MacArthur had started Kenney bombing the planes and ships and installations at Rabaul. During the whole of his desperate Buna campaign he had, time and again, plastered this key stronghold. He was to keep at it through all of 1943. Each time he moved Halsey's people northwestward, leap-frogging, by-passing, sliding off tackle, moving steadily forward in brilliant enveloping movements, Halsey could count on the Southwest Pacific's air taking long chances as they whittled away at Rabaul.

MacArthur's strategy was to move up these two shafts of the horseshoe, establish fighter bases within range of Rabaul, so that he could launch air strikes against this bastion with bombers protected by fighters. Once enemy air forces at Rabaul were neutralized, he could move simultaneously north along the New Guinea coast and the Solomons. He could capture the priceless

Key bases in the long campaign for the Solomons Sea and lower New Guinea.

Vitiaz Straits. Then he could take the Admiralties, neutralize New Ireland and establish control over the Bismarck Sea. He would then be free to move westward towards the Philippines.

The Japanese life lines that brought them in food, oil and bullets would then be cut, and the 150,000 Japanese left behind in sea camps and jungle islands would be surrounded and trapped. With supply and transportation denied them, their ultimate destruction became assured. Starvation, disease, bombing, blockade, all would combine to destroy them.

* * * *

MacArthur's left wing had first the difficult task of capturing the strong Japanese bases at Lae-Salamaua. He ordered Kenney to turn loose his bombers and secure control of the air. That was always the first MacArthur objective. It was far too costly to attempt to fight with his inadequate ground and sea forces while the enemy had control of the air. Kenney's bombers were his advance striking force. But bombers could only make daylight raids with minimum losses when they were protected by fighters.

The radius of his P-38's and P-47's was only three hundred miles at the most—so it was necessary to have fighter fields far ahead of the bomber strips. The long-range Forts could reach out eight hundred, or even a thousand miles, which was far beyond their fighter protectors. One of the major objectives of the next move was to advance the fighter line.

Carefully MacArthur laid out his plans for the Lae-Salamaua campaign. His partial air blockade of the sea routes to the Guinea coast had reduced the enemy's supplies to a dangerous level. He was certain that sooner or later his adversary must withdraw or make a major attempt to replenish his forces. MacArthur was positive he would do the latter.)

He called Kenney in and told him that within ten days the enemy would surely attempt a big relief convoy through the Bismarck Sea. Kenney was to be ready. He was to have Major General Whitehead gather every plane available for the strike and to prepare his tactical plan.

MacArthur felt the wily Japanese would wait for heavy weather and then under cover of a front try to sneak in. He was right—and Whitehead was ready. Under Kenney's directive he had carefully prepared and trained a special squadron of B-25's. These twelve—with Ed Larner in command—had been converted by the installation of additional armament into grim killers. In the nose of each were set eight 50-caliber machine guns—the deadliest quick-firing weapon in the world. When a pilot cut loose with his set of deadly toys he could saw a ship in two, slice a plane in half, or cut grass as clean as a lawn mower. Eight streams of white steel poured out of the nose of these vicious B-25's.

On February 27th the reconnaissance planes showed that the big Japanese convoy was about to move out of Rabaul. Our long-range weather man reported that the weather would be bad over the northern coast of New Britain, but good over the southeast coast. This meant that the enemy could move protected by a heavy weather front. The Nips had already gathered fighter planes at Lae, so that when the mists cleared they could give air coverage to the big convoy as it moved west and then south towards the New Guinea coast.

The convoy started, riding down from Rabaul under overcast skies. Our "recons" did their best to trail it throughout the night, but the drifting-cumulus hid the vessels from view. Around 7:30 that morning they picked up the convoy. Whitehead, Kenney's high-powered deputy, prepared for the kill. Every plane he could muster was alerted with the crew standing by. The Aussies contributed an experienced squadron of Beaufighters, and our own A-20's were fitted out to strafe as well as bomb. Kenney had been training his men in the deadly art of skip-bombing, and this day it was to prove its efficiency.

Whitehead made his calculations. By 10 that morning the convoy should be through the Vitiaz Straits and at an exact spot on the map. There he would hit them with everything he had.

His calculation was uncanny. At 10:05 his sky killers were over the spot—and the battle was on. In twenty minutes those vicious B-25's with their eight 50-caliber machine guns in each nose, took out ten Japanese ships. The Nip fighter cover did their best—but it simply wasn't good enough. Nothing could stop those A-20's and B-25's from tearing the heart out of those vessels. It was almost like shooting tame ducks in an Indiana pond.

Within 30 minutes after contact had been made, the Yanks had shot down 54 Nip planes, and long before darkness covered the appalling scene 12 Japanese transports and their 9 escorting war vessels had either been sent to the bottom or were getting ready to take the big dive. One destroyer managed somehow or other to limp away, but the next morning our planes located it, and quickly assisted the ship and crew to gain the immortality that comes through making the last sacrifice for the sacred Emperor.

When the final count was made our Trigger Boys had accounted for 102 planes out of the 150 Nip planes that had participated in the battle—and they had sunk 22 ships and some

15,000 men. There was little question that it would live as one of the epics of the whole war, and that its superb tactics would be studied for years to come.

Kenney himself left for Washington the day the action was concluded. His smile was not dissimilar to that of a satisfied cat that had just devoured the canary, when he read MacArthur's brilliant communique. "They didn't even leave six for pall-bearers," he grimly remarked.

Lae and Salamaua were now isolated and removed from all possible help. Squat little Japanese infantrymen, eating their half rations of rice and dried fish in their muddy gun pits and bomb shelters, would soon be growing hungry.

Their rice line had been cut. And so had their bullet line and their high octane gas line—and their reinforcement line, too.

And they soon were to have another costly lesson in MacArthur strategy.

* * * *

The main pillar of MacArthur's philosophy of modern war—fought with the barest forces and at the extreme minimum loss of human life—was his advancing bomber line protected by his short-range fighters. Operating once again on this sound principle, he now ordered Kenney to prepare forward fighter fields that could furnish his bombers protection while they pounded away at Rabaul and New Guinea bases and sea lanes.

Slowly MacArthur was evolving in his mind a plan first to by-pass this Jap stronghold of Lae and then pinch it off in a double envelopment movement. Australian infantry had for many months been in action in the Salamaua sector a little to the south.

The problem of supply then was a difficult one, and MacArthur ordered an abandoned strip at Wau—that had once been used by the gold mining people—fixed up so it could be used by Kenney's transports. The tough little Aussie garrison worried the Japs, and in January they attacked. By one of those split-second brushes with fate, it so happened that at the very moment when reinforcements were most needed several transports landed, and the Aussies poured out, firing as they hit the ground. The Japanese were driven back to Salamaua.

Now came the long, hard task of pushing on north, cutting temporary strips for the air transports and then converting them into permanent fighter fields. Just north of Marilinan, in the fantastic Markham Valley at Tsilli-Tsilli a fighter drome was planted. The Japs did not find out about this field until the middle of August. A good part of the late spring and early summer of 1943 was taken up with these operations. The jungle closed in on all sides. The sea was still dangerous, and the sky was only as safe as air patrols could make it. (Turn to map on page 111.)

On June 29th MacArthur struck from his right, his center, and his left simultaneously at widely separated objectives. Under cover of air and naval bombardment, amphibious forces of the distant right wing landed on New Georgia and Rendova Island—inaugurating the operations which finally resulted in envelopment of the Solomons. At the same time, from the center, bloodless landings were made in the Trobriands and Woodlark Island, east of lower New Guinea. Shortly, army Engineers (in the Trobriands) and Navy Seabees (on Woodlark) were to lay down airfields in record time, providing bases from which fighters could give protection to long-range bomber attacks. In these amphibious operations, MacArthur for the first time used and tested LCI's and LST's and other amphibious equipment which was later used on a vastly greater scale in the European theater.

Amphibious engineers now landed American ground troops at Nassau Bay on up the north coast of New Guinea; they were soon to join the Australians advancing overland on Mubo and thus pave the way for the eventual capture of Salamaua.

The Japanese didn't catch on, but MacArthur had started the great wheeling movement, and within nine months' time he was to neutralize and by-pass the strong enemy positions here on the north, and then ultimately turn his full force westward—towards the Philippines.

Always our air was pounding away at that great Japanese base at Rabaul. The success of operations on both sides of the giant six-hundred-mile-wide nutcracker, depended largely on neutralizing the Nip bombers there both before and during the landing operations.

Meanwhile the legendary Colonel Jock Sverdrup had been flown to a tiny goldfield strip far to the northwest at Bena-Bena—a land a mile high and a million miles wide. From here he and a curious explorer named Mick Lehary, of the Royal Australian Air Force, slogged it over to the Markham River, and then followed this strange and beautiful valley to a spot called Nadzab.

Here they picked an area that was soon destined to become one of the most fantastic air centers in the world. From its conception to its full growth it was a storybook creation—as unreal as the mists and thunderheads of the Kokoda trail or the legends of American mystery subs from Australian and other Pacific bases that were sinking a hundred times their weight in enemy ships.

To the north of this point of Nadzab in the rich Markham

Valley was the Japanese base of Wewak, and on to the east mighty Rabaul. These were the two great air bases of the enemy. Together they represented a much greater force than we could muster. But with Nadzab in being MacArthur would then have his one main base midway between the two, and he could concentrate first on the one and then the other. In this way, in spite of his inferior numbers he hoped to attain air mastery by fighting his divided enemy one at a time. It was Napoleon and his Italy campaign all over again, but transferred to the new medium of the air.

Since his immediate ground objective was Lae, he planned first to neutralize Wewak, on the north. In a series of brilliant surprise blows in middle August, our air blasted this great base with its four fields into operative helplessness. Hundreds of Japanese planes were caught on the ground and destroyed, and the enemy was forced to pull back its air support more than three hundred miles to Hollandia. The way was now cleared. Our air force faced only Rabaul.

MacArthur moved swiftly. In a coordinated ground, air and naval operation, the 9th Australian Division—the beloved "Rats of Tobruk"—were successfully landed on the coast northeast of Lae, cutting the enemy's main line of communication and supply from the north. The movement was a complete surprise and the landing was made with little opposition. The troops came ashore under cover of a smoke screen following a naval bombardment and protected by air formations.

The investment of the Lae-Salamaua area was now well under way. It was the first of a series of beautifully executed amphibious operations that were to follow one another like turning pages of history—Hopi Bay, Finschhafen, Arawe, Gloucester, Saidor, the

Admiralties, the 500-mile leap to Hollandia in April, 1944, and in the following May and June to stab on up the Guinea coast to Wakde and Biak. (Turn back to map on page 111.)

MacArthur's amphibious commander was an admirable sailor, Rear Admiral Barbey. From now on he was to head up MacArthur's swift-moving, high-scoring 7th Amphibious Force. This, too, was limited in size, but somehow it always came through, with an unbelievably small loss of life. "Uncle Dan" Barbey had the MacArthur touch there. He knew the art of perfect timing.

With the Aussies safely landed at Hopi Bay, MacArthur figured out with Kenney that the Japanese would at once shoot out their planes from Rabaul. Carefully they set their air trap. High in the sky, with the sun to their back, the deadly Yank fighters made their rendezvous. The Rabaul dive bombers sailed straight into it. It was shooting clay pigeons for the Yanks. In less than that many minutes they sent 41 Nip planes screaming to the earth or into the Bay. Not a single Nip plane got home to its nest.

The next day MacArthur closed the ring on Lae and Salamaua. In a comprehensive air movement he landed an American paratroop regiment, with Australian artillery, at Nadzab, and seized the inland approaches along the wide Markham Valley. The operation completely surprised the enemy's ground troops engaged on the other fronts by our encircling forces. Elements of four Japanese divisions, of an aggregate strength of 20,000, were now enveloped, with no hope of supply.

The action had all the elements of a great movie spectacle. From 9 fields a total of 305 planes sailed into the blue, and set their course for the lovely Markham Valley. Ahead rode five squadrons of proud B-25's, with their noses full of those wicked

50-caliber machine guns. They came sixteen abreast like white circus horses. They cut the grass and cleaned out every living thing in their path.

Next marched 12 A-20's, laying down three lanes of smoke; between them came the 96 C-47 transport planes, in three columns of thirty-two transports each. At their head drove a gleaming combat Flying Fortress. Inside it was a tall, quiet soldier, who wore an old cap, heavily embroidered in gold.

His staff had tried their best to dissuade him from going in, but MacArthur said he would lead the way for his paratroopers. It was their first fight and "he would give them such comfort as his presence might mean to them." And now the white puffs dropped quickly out of the great sky transports—hundreds of American paratroopers from the far-away cities and towns and farms of America.

In exactly one minute and ten seconds the paratroopers contacted the earth—and the land was theirs. Then out tumbled a full battery of General Blamey's splendid artillery, with their 25-pounders—four-inch guns—sailing gracefully earthward under their own silk parachutes. The ammunition followed them to the good earth.

As the men and their guns floated gracefully down through warm skies, they could see a flight of 27 great Liberators bombing Heath's Plantation, where the enemy might be lurking. There would be no surprise attacks from that direction.

"Make it safe from air attacks," MacArthur had warned Kenney time and again. Kenney did make it safe. Those Yanks and Aussies sliding down the sky chutes could see 64 friendly Yank and Aussie fighters riding each flank, 2,000 feet above the earth. Eight thousand feet above, other fighter groups watched the far reaches of the high horizons. And at 20,000 feet still another group combed the distances for enemies. It was a sight for the gods.

Trailing behind them all came 5 special Forts, with their bomb racks loaded with 300-pound bags of various supplies, each tied to its own parachute. By simple panel arrangements the ground troops could signal for exactly the type of supplies they needed; and the pilot by pulling a certain lever could let that particular bundle drop like a feather in the wind to the earth.

That night MacArthur radioed back this assurance to his anxious wife in Brisbane, "It was a honey."

Salamaua, south of Lae, would fall one week to a day after the winged men had dropped down out of the skies on Nadzab. Encircling arms would close tight around doomed Lae; arms from the east and west and south.

And in September MacArthur could announce his first great offensive victory—the capture of the Japanese base at Lae.

* * * *

Like a ball rolling down a hillside, American Engineers along with 500 of General Blamey's thin-bellied Aussies, rolled on northward up the Markham Valley. At Kaiapit they hurriedly hacked out a temporary field; then they jumped for a wide flat area, perfect for another great air base. It was to be known by the odd name of Gusap.

It lay in the jungle—as impenetrable to men on foot as if it were an island in a great sea. Here a military city of several thousands of people was soon to spring into life. Every pound of supplies and matériel had to be flown in to it. Rather than load the air transports with lumber, Kenney shipped in a dismantled sawmill, and Casey's engineers set it up, cut the trees, sawed the lumber and built the hundreds of buildings.

MacArthur's bomber line had been pushed forward another 300 miles by this great fighter drome here at isolated, jungle-ringed Gusap. It had been built well and strong. That is the MacArthur way of doing things. Always the air bases must be sturdy and sufficient. For this strange war in the far Pacific is a war of supply lines. And these supply lines are largely controlled from the air.

To an almost unbelievable degree air mastery has meant jungle and sea mastery. When an operation was being considered, MacArthur made certain that he had air mastery. It was the first prerequisite. For without air control, victory could only be secured at a price far greater in human life than MacArthur was willing to pay.

And he had no spare ships to lose, oil to waste, guns to throw away, supplies to squander. While other theaters could go about their war in the grand manner, he must stint and save and add together, holding back his strikes until his meager reserves gave him a chance.

* * * *

Affairs in the country that Halsey had borrowed from MacArthur on the great eastern prong of the nut-cracker, were going ahead slowly but surely. The rugged old sea dog was also operating on a shoestring—with now and again a special task force of carriers and cruisers and amphibious equipment that Nimitz would lend him.

The area Halsey was operating in was quite different from the New Guinea country where MacArthur's Yank and Aussie doughboys and fliers, and his 7th Amphibian Force, were methodi-

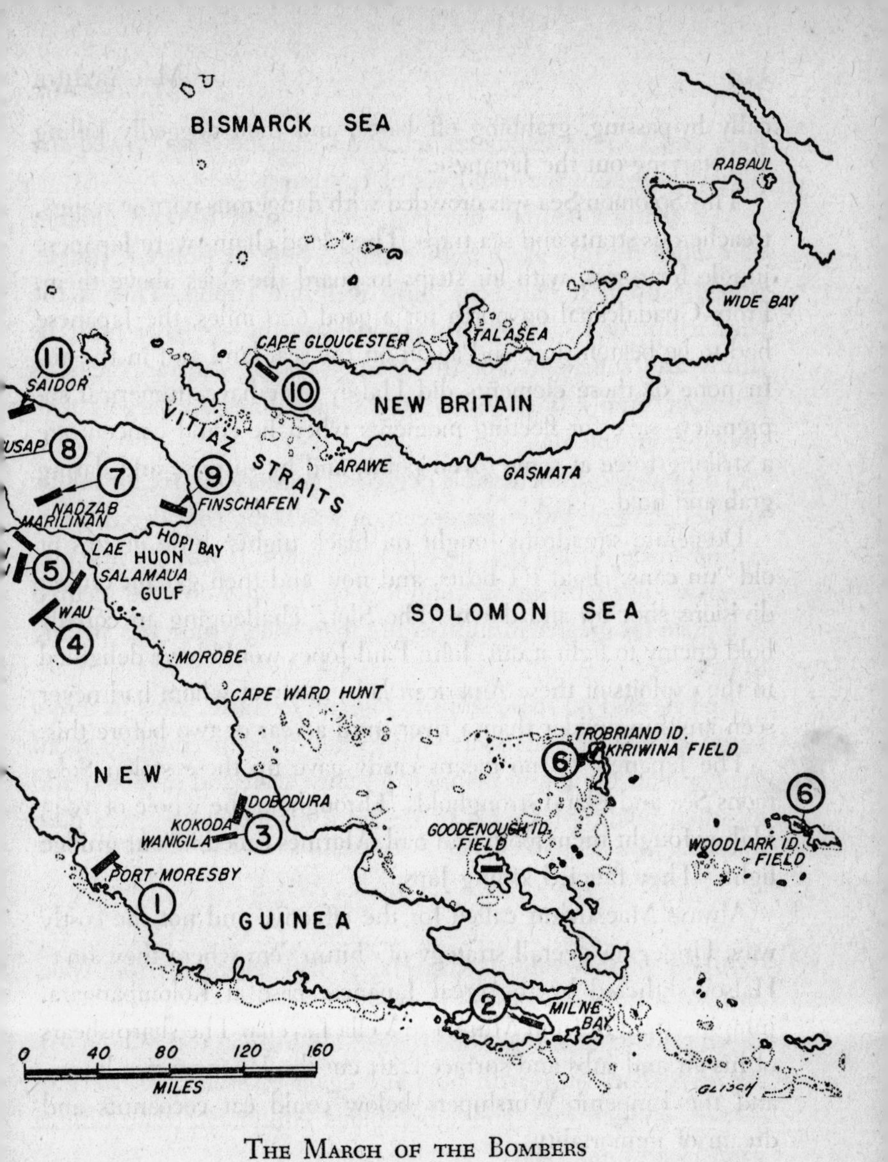

The March of the Bombers

[H]ow the advancing air bases moved with deadly rhythm, steadily pushing back the enemy lines.

cally by-passing, grabbing off bases, and then doggedly killing and starving out the Japanese.

This Solomon Sea was crowded with dangerous narrow waters, treacherous straits and sea traps. The island chains were Japanese jungle fortresses, with air strips to guard the skies above them. From Guadalcanal on north for a good 600 miles, the Japanese had to be beaten time and again on the sea, land and in the air. In none of these elements did Halsey ever have numerical supremacy—save for fleeting moments when he could concentrate a striking force at some given point, and by surprise and daring grab and hold.

Desperate squadrons fought on black nights; little groups of old "tin cans," bold PT-boats, and now and then gallant cruiser divisions shot up and down "The Slot," challenging an equally bold enemy to fight it out. John Paul Jones would have delighted in the exploits of these American lads, many of whom had never seen anything wider than a river until a year or two before this.

The Japanese by no means easily gave up these stolen Solomons Sea and island strongholds. Throughout the whole of 1943 Halsey fought them tooth and nail. Marines called it "our grudge fight." They fancied killing Japs.

Always MacArthur called for the effective and not the costly way. Under his overall strategy of "hittin' 'em where they ain't" Halsey slithered by the great Japanese base at Kolombangara, jumping straight from Munda to Vella Lavella. The sharp shears of his air and subs and surface craft cut the Japanese rice lines—and the Emperor Worshipers below could eat cocoanuts and dream of immortality.

On to the north was a great Japanese concentration in the Buin-Faisi area, at the lower end of the sprawling island of Bougainville. Possibly 20,000 Nips patiently awaited here the coming of the hated Americans. It was a road block to the northern drive of the Yanks.

MacArthur badly needed an air base southeast of New Britain, so that his fighter-escorted bombers could keep pounding away at Rabaul, still the key to all the Japanese defenses in the Solomons and Bismarck Seas. By a queer phenomenon of weather there were certain times of the year when heavy cloud banks swept the skies to the south and west of Rabaul, cutting off all air attacks from the Guinea dromes. At other times of the year the weather front hung to the southeast of Rabaul, down towards the Bougainville country.

In order to keep the fighter-escorted bombers constantly working on Rabaul, MacArthur must have a great air base somewhere here to the southeast in Bougainville, so that when Kenney's air was cut off by fog from the west, the skies to the southeast would be clear for bombers coming up from below. It was absolutely necessary to get a southern bomber and fighter base, and MacArthur ordered Halsey to capture or make one. (Turn back to map on page 111.)

But that heavy Japanese fist at the lower tip of Bougainville was blocking the way. Halsey was directed to by-pass the mighty base at Buin-Faisi, swing to the westward of the great island of Bougainville under the cover of darkness, and then strike into Empress Augusta Bay at dawn.

But before doing so MacArthur would clear the air at Rabaul for him. Kenney, Whitehead, Cooper, the entire air force, American and Australian, gathered themselves for the mighty blow which fell in mid-October. With complete secrecy the mass of our air force was concentrated and launched from fields built in the captured portions of New Guinea that we had occupied late in June.

The dividing of the Nip air forces into two great groups based upon Wewak and Rabaul had made it possible to use our main mass against first one flank and then the other, thus acquiring in each case superiority of force at the point of combat, and destroying the enemy's force in detail.

The surprise at Rabaul was as complete as it had been at Wewak. With every available plane in line we struck at midday. The enemy was caught completely unaware, with his planes, both bombers and fighters, on the ground. While our medium bombers raked the airdromes, our heavies pounded the shipping in the harbor. Both groups were covered by our fighters. Our low-flying medium bombers, striking at the three big airdromes, destroyed 100 enemy aircraft caught on the ground, and severely damaged 51 others.

Forty Nip fighters were able to take to the air and of these 26 were shot down in combat. In all 177 airplanes, or approximately sixty percent of the enemy's total air strength at this base, was lost to him in the blistering attack. Operations buildings, radio installations, and many fuel and ammunition dumps were demolished or heavily damaged; antiaircraft positions were silenced and a motor transport pool was wrecked—and all at a cost of five planes missing and a few damaged.

It was a shellacking that the Japanese were never to forget. Along with the knocking out of the enemy at Wewak, it gave us definite mastery in the air over the Solomons Sea and adjacent waters, and threatened the entire Japanese outer defensive perimeter in the Bismarck and Solomon Seas.

In the battle operation room of the Air Force in New Guinea, where he had been intently following the operation, General MacArthur warmly congratulated his senior air commander. "Rabaul has been the center and very hub of the enemy's advanced air effort," he continued; "I think we have now broken its back."

The aftermath was to prove how definitely he had actually "broken its back." Again and again the enemy was to make frantic efforts to rebuild this great citadel of the air at Rabaul. To this front he was to fly not only his base reserves, but he was to strip his mandated islands of their air potential and thereby expose himself to the swift stroke which followed in due course from the main Pacific Fleet of Nimitz.

To this Rabaul front the Nips practically committed the air forces of their Empire, only to see them again and again whittled away in detail by the relentless air groups of the South and Southwest Pacific. All was in vain. Rabaul became the graveyard of their air hopes. MacArthur on that bright October day truly "broke its back."

The sea was now cleared, and Halsey's planners borrowed carriers and a formidable task force, and quietly gathered together a mighty armada for the attack on Empress Augusta Bay. Kenney, far to the west, once again plastered Rabaul, and there was little coming out of the skies to oppose the American landing made halfway up the west coast of the 200-mile-long island of Bougainville.

But there was plenty of danger coming down on the sea from Rabaul. A force of heavy cruisers and destroyers suddenly broke out from the Jap base and headed southeastward.

Halsey, anticipating this move, ordered Rear Admiral Tip Merril to meet the enemy with our task force. Rugged old Halsey's radio order will live as long as the American Fleet exists. It is probably the shortest operation order ever written and it meant exactly what it said: "Interpose your force between the enemy and the convoy. And if you meet him, you know what to do."

Tip Merril did meet the enemy and he knew what to do. In six hours of high-speed action, part of it in darkness, he chased the enemy home, and on the way sank seven cruisers and destroyers. All threat of Japanese naval interference to the landings at Empress Bay was now removed.

Troops, guns and supplies poured ashore. American patrols swung far out into the jungle, so there would be sufficient room within the outer perimeter for the air strips. Seabees rushed in with their bulldozers, and a fighter airfield came to life. It would be the sole job of these tough Marines and equally tough Doughboys to guard this strip. That was their main mission in life, once the landing had been made. It was the new tactics of sea, air and jungle fighting.

The once treacherous jungle that for so long had been the enemy of MacArthur's Doughboys and Vandegrift's Marines, here and over in Guinea and everywhere, was now to become their friend and protector. The tables were reversed at last; no longer would Americans and Aussies have to cut their trails through the jungle to get at the enemy; the enemy now had to battle his way through the rain forests, the poisonous swamps, the devastating high passes, swim rivers in flood, and fight hunger and fever, to reach our outposts. We were now the masters of the jungle.

Torpedo boats and subs and tireless bombers could now cut the Japanese chow line, and high octane line, the ammunition line far ahead—and the tens of thousands of Japanese left behind,

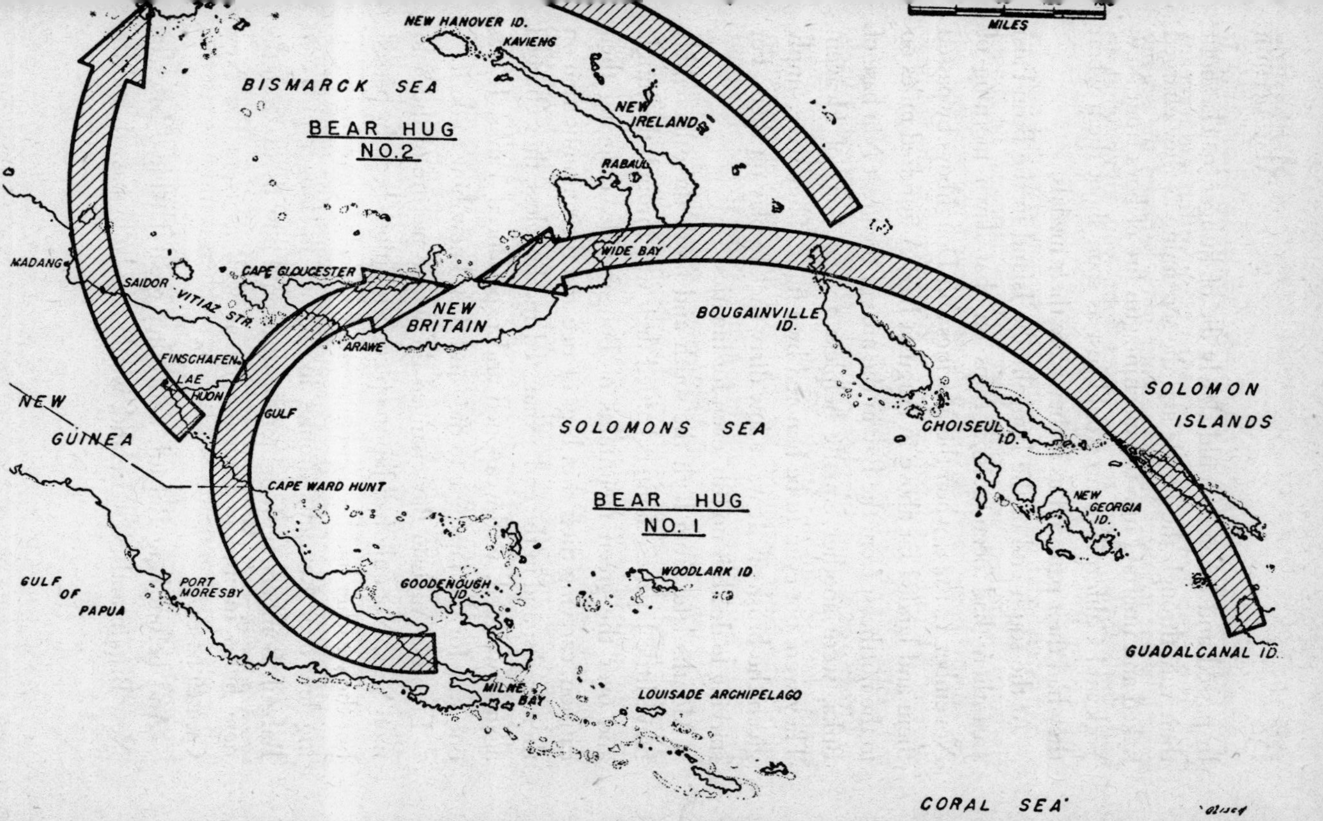

The two great enveloping moves, or Bear Hugs, that in 1943 and early 1944 netted MacArthur the Solomons and the Bismarck Sea.

by-passed and ignored, could slowly die of hunger; or else fight their way through the jungle and die screaming as they charged naked and unafraid into the machine-gun fire of boys from New York and California—who would just as soon shoot them when they had their pants off as if they wore their medals.

At the south end of the Bougainville Island in the Buin-Faisi area there had been 20,000 Nips on that dawn morning of November 1, 1943, when the Marines and Doughboys by-passed them and landed far above in Augusta Bay. A hundred miles on to the northeast from the Bay in the area of the great Nip base of Buka, were another equally helpless 20,000 Sons of Heaven. They were not even to be honored by a fight. They were simply given the brush-off. It was a low dirty trick to play on them. For starving to death is no fun, even for fanatics.

Months later from both the south and north these incredibly brave little Japanese fighters battled their way through the jungle and over the green mountains of Bougainville, dragging their cannon, carrying their thin bags of rice and their ammunition on their backs; and in the end, exhausted and hopeless, they charged against well-fed, well-weaponed and experienced Yanks. It was one way for the Japanese to die—and they knew how to do it.

Empress Augusta Bay changed the whole picture of the Solomon Seas. Not only had Jap troop concentrations been by-passed, but the weather had been circumvented, as well. Those fogs hanging low over Kenney's dromes in Guinea no longer protected Rabaul. Bombers, with fighter escorts, could now fly up from the new fields in middle Bougainville as well as from the New Guinea bases.

And before long Rabaul, and other great Japanese bases on New Britain and New Ireland, would also be by-passed, and the chow lines and gas lines cut. And more than 150,000 enraged and helpless Nips left behind could carry on their losing war against the female mosquito. Hunger and fever, the pitiless jungle and the sea and sky, all were their enemies now.

Great Bear Hug Number One was ended.

CHAPTER EIGHT

MacARTHUR ALWAYS CAREFULLY PREPARED FOR THE KILL. His three principles of war were simple and fundamental. First, there must be adequate bases; then sound planning; and third, bold execution. His fairly small staff at Headquarters was fully indoctrinated with these principles. His was always the overall strategy, and once he made his decision he did not care to be bothered with details. He kept his time and mental energy for the big job. He did not clutter up his mind or hours with little things that other men could do. He had true perspective. It was part of his military genius.

Another important factor was the talent he had of getting along with difficult people in trying situations. He had hewn to the line from that historic moment on March 26, 1942, when he had put his hand on John Curtin's shoulder and said solemnly and fervently, "Mr. Prime Minister, you and I will see this thing through together."

It had been no easy matter to keep in proper balance the Australian War Council, the Opposition leaders, and the rank and file of the Army, and the seven million people of this enormous continent. The three experienced divisions of the Australian Imperial Forces were composed of proud and able men. General Sir Thomas Blamey was a four-star General in his own right, with a breast full of ribbons. But from his first conference with MacArthur this old warrior recognized that the American was a man of high character, unimpeachable honor, and a great professional soldier. Blamey did not mind serving under him. And neither did his rugged, rangy, singing soldiers—the magnificent Diggers. They were never to mistrust for a second MacArthur's leadership. He was never to let them down. He knew their great qualities and how to get the level best out of them. The respect and admiration were mutual.

MacArthur always saw to it that he knew not only his own men, but as well his enemy. From 1905, when he had been Aide to his father, then the Chief American Observer with Oyama's army in Manchuria, Douglas MacArthur had studied Japanese character and ambitions. Through the years he watched the steady, compelling development of the fanatical Japanese national religion. He knew how powerful it was in its indoctrinations. He realized fully what it would mean to fight an army of Japanese fanatics, who were willing to die without complaint for their Emperor and their regiment. Death was their reward—bravery their commonplace virtue. Here lay the Japanese strength.

But MacArthur knew equally well where their weakness lay. So imbued were they with their mad Shintoism that they were totally unprepared even to think of defeat. It was against the tenacity of their politico-religion to plan great withdrawals and progressive lines of retreat. They had been taught from childhood they were completely invincible. They could not spell "defeat." For them there was honor only in death. Gladly they would die charging against machine guns, seeking immortality in death for their Emperor. The emphasis was not on a desire to live. Rather they wanted to die nobly.

It was a brutalized philosophy that encompassed all ranks. It didn't matter how a Japanese died, as long as he was snuffed out fighting. Death and not victory was the final reward. Americans and Europeans might jestingly say, "He who fights and runs away lives to fight another day." But that was far beyond these religion-inspired Japanese to understand, even as a joke.

MacArthur knew that his enemy was psychologically incapable of withdrawing from the bases of his defense perimeter, even when he saw he faced positive defeat. MacArthur was sure that he would not have to fight the same Japanese troops time after time in new battlegrounds; he knew they would *not* withdraw, make fresh stands, withdraw again, to make another and another stand.

A quarter-million brave Japanese soldiers, well-equipped, well-supplied and well-entrenched, faced him. Some of them he would have to fight and kill where they stood. There was no question about that; when his men joined battle with them they had to kill them. They never surrendered, and in the whole first two years of the Pacific campaign he was actually to capture less than a thousand unwounded men.

But the majority of that quarter-million he could by-pass, isolate and thus assure their ultimate destruction with minimum loss to himself.

Tojo had simply spread his front lines too wide and too far away. Ole Debil Distance would get him in the end. It was impossible for this far-flung Japanese line to be strong everywhere. And by picking the spot, by-passing the strong points, and "hittin' 'em where they ain't," MacArthur could get in front of their bases. Then by controlling the air and the sea and undersea he could cut their grocery lines and starve them to death. It was as simple as that to MacArthur.

Their stubborn, dumb refusal to anticipate defeat and withdraw to new battlegrounds, was to backfire in the very face of

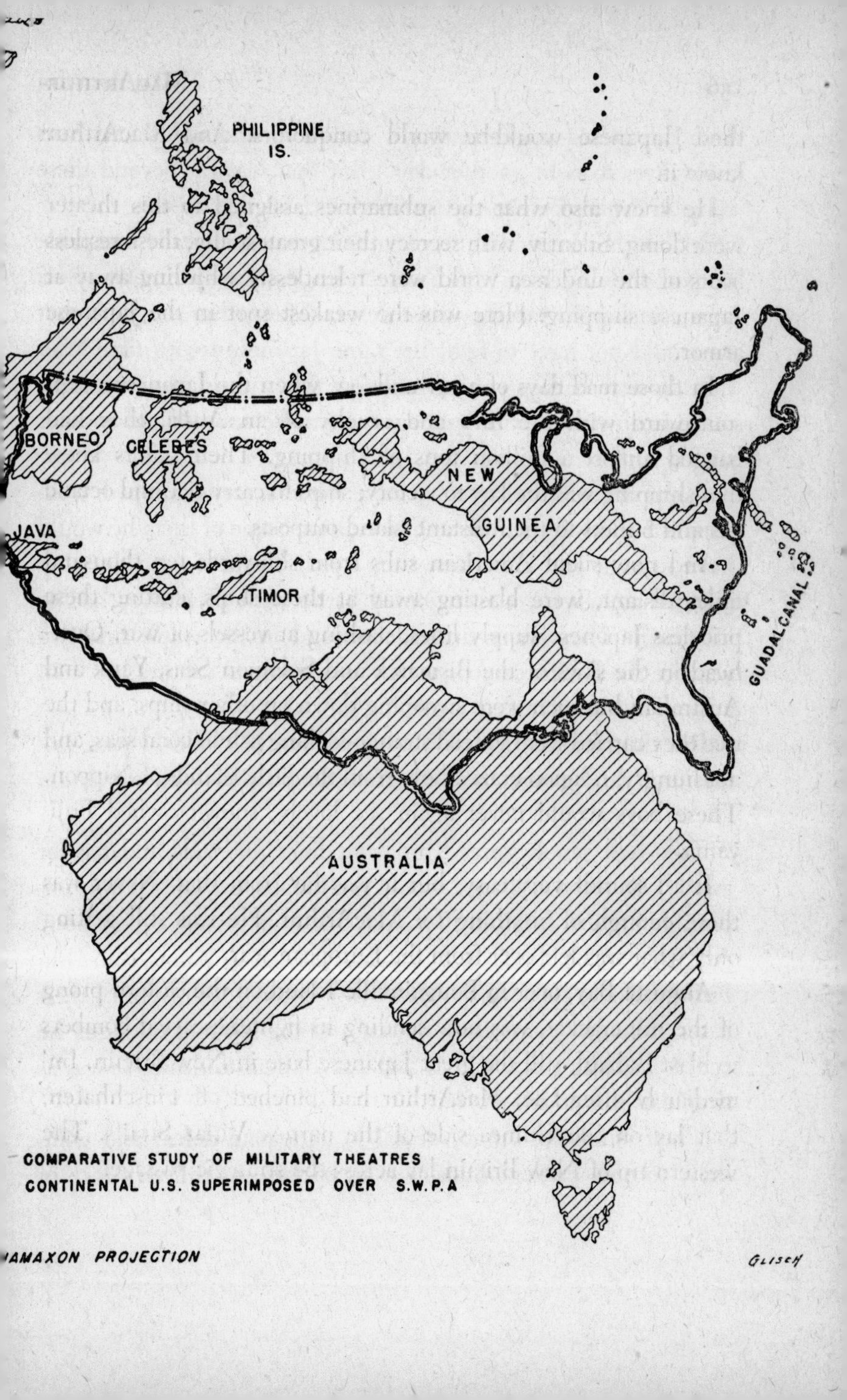

COMPARATIVE STUDY OF MILITARY THEATRES
CONTINENTAL U.S. SUPERIMPOSED OVER S.W.P.A

AMAXON PROJECTION

these Japanese would-be world conquerors. And MacArthur knew it.

He knew also what the submarines assigned to this theater were doing. Silently, with secrecy their greatest ally, these restless boats of the undersea world were relentlessly whittling away at Japanese shipping. Here was the weakest spot in the Japanese armor.

In those mad days of 1941 and '42, when the Japanese swept southward with the fury and cruelty of an Attila, they had bagged almost a million tons of shipping. Their sailors knew that shipping was the key to victory; ships to carry rice and octane gas and bullets to their distant island outposts.

And now silent American subs from shipyards ten thousand miles distant, were blasting away at these ships, cutting these priceless Japanese supply lines, slashing at vessels of war. Overhead in the skies of the Bismarck and Solomon Seas, Yank and Australian birdmen were swooping down on other ships; and the rice they carried went to feed strange-looking fish in coral seas, and not hungry, religion-crazed boys from the little islands of Nippon. These boys would never again see lovely, snow-crowned Fujiyama.

It all sounds very easy, but it was far from that. Never was there enough of anything for MacArthur. He was still getting only what was left over from the European war.

Augusta Bay, over in Bougainville Island on the eastern prong of the nut-cracker, was now sending its fighter-escorted bombers to blast Rabaul, still the great Japanese base in New Britain. Immediately after Lae, MacArthur had pinched off Finschhafen, that lay on the Guinea side of the narrow Vitiaz Straits. The western tip of New Britain lay across the strategic passage.

This sixty-mile-wide body of water was the shuttle that ran between the Solomon Sea and the Bismarck Sea above New Britain. Before he could send his ships and loading barges with safety into this new northern country, MacArthur must gain control of these vital Vitiaz Straits. Strike after strike was made on Rabaul. But though the Nips there were tough and experienced and constantly receiving air replacements, the deadly threat of the Rabaul sky raiders was growing weaker and weaker. MacArthur had "broken its back."

On December 15th, 1943, Krueger's dismounted horsemen of the 112th Cavalry Regiment, with Brigadier General Cunningham in charge of the ground fighters, landed on the long neck of land that called itself Arawe Peninsula, on the lower east shore of Vitiaz Straits. Kenney's bombers had blasted and pasted the beaches and destroyers had shelled the shore, but there were still Nips there, and the fighting was sharp. But Arawe was in reality only a diversion to draw the attention of the Japanese away from Gloucester—the true objective. (Map on page 111.)

This Krueger was a real soldier, too. He and MacArthur were old comrades. Krueger was a year younger than MacArthur and shared the same birthday. MacArthur had hand-picked him, and set him up in charge of his brand-new Sixth Army. He wore three stars, and he was hard and experienced and talented; old Walter Krueger, born in Germany, brought up in the plains of Nebraska. He had fought his way up from buck private to lieutenant general. MacArthur never had to tell him more than once what he wanted done.

With Arawe in the bag, MacArthur now threw his energy into the final plans of the battle for Gloucester, nestling at the northeast point of the Vitiaz Straits where it debouches into the

Bismarck Sea. Here at Gloucester he would use the First Marine Division, Vandegrift's old outfit, now under Major General Bill Rupertus.

He ordered Kenney to start the shellacking. It was music to Kenney's ears. Killing Nips had got to be his trade. His boys didn't mind either.

Photographs showed Gloucester had an air strip some five miles up from the best landing beach, with a road paralleling the shore leading to it. Back from this road were the supply dumps hidden in the jungle. The dispersion area for the planes backed off from the strip. Kenney's job was to destroy the strip and any planes nearby; blast the trail and supply dumps; and lastly, help clean up any Japanese resistance on the landing beaches after the barking guns of the escorting warships of the 7th Amphibious Fleet had quieted down.

MacArthur picked the day after Christmas. Somehow he simply couldn't order an attack to start on the sacred day itself. That morning he sent to his troops one of those exquisite moving messages that few living men can so perfectly phrase. It came from deep down in his heart:

"To the Fighting Forces of the Southwest Pacific Area:

"On this Christmas Day, the anniversary of the birth of cur Lord, Jesus Christ, I pray that a merciful God may preserve and bless each one of you."

* * * *

First of all Kenney's strafers and light bombers cut to ribbons the trail and the country for a hundred yards behind. Those hard B-25's with the eight 50-caliber machine guns in their noses, largely took care of that chore. Then he moved on over to the airfield. Flying twelve abreast on each side of the drome, the strafers cut their clean swathes, row on row outside the strip. For a hundred yards back of the edges of the field there wasn't a mosquito alive. Then the killers shifted to the strip itself.

Heavy bombers flying low tore the face off the surface of the field with their 1,000- and 2,000-pound bombs. Back and forth they went. Then the mediums and the strafers worked their deadly pattern criss-cross from one corner of the field to the other—just in case some AA gun or machine gun nest was left. When this fellow Kenney took out a drome he really took it out.

This, of course, was all preliminary to the actual landings. Kenney helped cover this as an old hen covers her baby chicks when a rain comes. His lifting, rolly sky barrages advanced with the precision of land artillery. He bombed and strafed and tore the heart out of everything on and back of the actual beaches—everything that the bombardment of the escorting warships had left alone.

The 1st Marine Division—the grand First of Guadalcanal—rushed the landing beaches with no initial loss at all. The air and the Navy had swept the beach-heads for them. Thirty-five hundred Japanese was the toll taken before the actual landings began. The remaining 3,500 were so slap-happy that "Jungle Jim" Whaling, and his hard-hitting 1st Marine Regiment, quickly pushed up to the air strip and beyond, set their machine guns, emplaced their 105 howitzers and were ready for the mad rushes by the time the Nips could crawl out of the jungle and set themselves for their counter-charges. The rain forests and the mosquitoes got the few the Marines failed to kill.

With the speed of lightning MacArthur then struck back at Guinea, across the Vitiaz Straits, to trap the enemy forces slowly retreating along the Huon Peninsula coast in front of the advancing Australians from Finschhafen. Instantly organizing an amphibious force of the same type used at Arawe and Gloucester, he seized Saidor with its airfield, and trapped thousands of the enemy. The surprise was complete and his losses negligible. With their supplies gone, and Australian bayonets at their rear, the Japanese took to the deadly jungles. Soon their emaciated bodies studded the trails like the signboards of a town road. No more descriptive story of privation and starvation has ever been written in the history of war. The entire Huon Peninsula was now MacArthur's.

The first of his great double encirclements was over. The Solomons Sea had now become a friendly lake. Tens of thousands of Japanese and a dozen and more complete dromes were still alive on its fringes and on its jungle islands. But they belonged to the mosquitoes and the crocodiles. They were the hostages of Fate. Their great strongholds had become Hunger Forts.

MacArthur could now swiftly turn to his second classic double envelopment. (Turn back to map on page 129.)

* * * *

The Bismarck Sea is a great oval roughly 600 miles from east to west and some 300 miles from north to south. To the south is the quarter-moon shaped island of New Britain. At its eastern tip is the key fortress of Rabaul, and extending northwest from it is the cigar-shaped island of New Ireland. This big island of New Ireland, and a group of scattered dots above it, form the outer eastern edge of the Bismarck Sea. The southwest boundary is the vast, impenetrable shore of New Guinea. To the north lie the scattered Admiralty Islands.

Rabaul, in the southern edge of the Bismarck Sea, was now almost eliminated as an enemy striking base. The powerful Japanese airfield at Kavieng, in the northern tip of New Ireland, was also largely neutralized. On the Guinea side MacArthur had planted an advance fighter field at Saidor to protect Kenney's bombers. But the Japanese still held their strong points in those Admiralties to the north. And MacArthur would have to pinch these out before he could really claim this Bismarck Sea as his own—and then move on down the Long Road back to the Philippines.

The first job was for Halsey to grab little Green Island, off the lower tip of New Ireland. This helped to isolate Rabaul. The next job was the occupation of Emirau Island that would neutralize Kavieng. There were no losses. These quick moves meant that great Rabaul, which for a year and a half had been the menacing stronghold and stumbling block for all this part of the Pacific world, would soon be by-passed, humiliated, thumbed-to-nose. Kavieng was likewise eliminated.

MacArthur would in the end dismiss Rabaul without the cost of a single doughboy. He'd simply pass it up; and what was left of that original 70,000 Japanese garrison force on New Britain could learn to live without food.

Previous to all this, Nimitz had started his amphibious sweeps straight across the central Pacific from Pearl Harbor. He had taken the Gilberts, overrun and by-passed the Marshalls, and raided the Japanese base at Truk. By pure hard luck he missed a whack at a part of the Japanese Grand Fleet that long had based there.

Halsey's long-distance reconnaissance planes fanned out from their New Georgia base, guarding against surprise coming down from above. MacArthur's right and upper flanks were now protected. He had plans all drawn for a full-scale, overwhelming assault on the Admiralties—the islands that held the key that would open the door to the northern waters that stretched out to the Philippines.

Kenney sent over his "recon's" and the pictures showed that the air strip at Momote, in the tiny island of Los Negros, had little signs of planes and evidences of only a few Japanese. Just to the westward was the larger island of Manus, with a second strip. Other intelligence reports from MacArthur's G-2 stubbornly insisted that in the group of islands there were still some 4,000 Japanese. But a quick surprise landing might catch them napping.

MacArthur leaped like a panther. Cancelling the elaborate plans for a great attack scheduled to come a month later, he gathered together a light naval force of two cruisers and twelve destroyers, and a handful of transports, with a single reinforced squadron of the 5th U. S. Cavalry aboard. Tough old I. P. Swift, Commanding General of the 1st U. S. Cavalry Division, sent along his senior Brigade Commander, William C. Chase.

With the sixth sense that all great generals must at times show, MacArthur had had a strange hunch that he might be needing some such swiftly organized spearhead, and he had kept the boats and men ready to shove off at a moment's notice. So it was that he could order into action this surprise expedition without the slightest delay. And in reserve, with steam up, he had sufficient power to back his spearhead if any large enemy mass was hurled against him.

On the cruiser going north that night of February 29th, his Aide, Col. Larry Lehrbas, had casually mentioned to the General that such few troops as he was sending ashore had never been in actual combat, and consequently might not do as well as he was counting on.

The General looked out over the darkened sea and an odd look came in his eyes. "I have known this 5th Cavalry for sixty years," he said slowly. "When I was a little boy of four my father was a Captain in the 13th Infantry, stationed at Fort Selden in the Indian frontier of New Mexico. Geronimo, the Apache scourge, was loose, and our little infantry garrison was to guard the upper fords of the Rio Grande. A troop of this same 5th Cavalry under Henry Lawton—later killed as a Major General in the Philippines—with Charles King, later famed as a military author, as his Lieutenant, rode through to help us. I can still remember how I felt when I watched them clatter into the fort, their tired horses gray with the desert dust. . . . They'd fight then—and they'll fight now. Don't worry about them, Larry."

And fight they did. This sturdy old 1st Cavalry Division was the only outfit MacArthur had been given up to this time that still had a heavy seasoning of old Regulars. And they had tradition and a steadiness, and they did not know fear.

The cruisers and the destroyers blasted away at the landing beach for a few minutes, and in the murky drizzle of early morning the four dismounted troops, with a battery of mountain guns and another of antiaircraft, jumped out of their landing barges and hit the beach. The surprise was so complete, and the plan so audacious and unbelievable, that hardly a corporal's guard immediately opposed them.

MacArthur came ashore in an open landing boat wearing his old gold-embroidered cap, now worn and soiled. Some young officer worried for the general's safety saluted and warned him that the Jap snipers were operating just forward. "Where?" said the general, moving in that direction.

The three or four officers and the handful of cavalrymen who walked ahead with him were astounded and thrilled at his total disregard of danger. The men wore steel helmets and the splotched green battle-dress that makes them almost a part of the jungle. MacArthur wore a light trench coat and his Lucky Cap—a clear-cut target for snipers.

A few days later Lt. Colonel Jane Clement, Chief of the 3,500 army nurses in the theater, visited an advanced hospital on the Guinea coast, where the battle casualties from the Admiralties had been sent. As was her invariable custom she called on every wounded man, and brought to him the solace of a great-hearted motherly woman. At one cot she held the hand of a boy who had been badly machine-gunned. He would get well, but he would never walk unaided again. He listened to Jane's brave words of encouragement, then he broke in: "Say 'Ma', you should have seen the General—he was right up there with us."

"You mean General Chase?" Jane questioned.

"No, no," the boy insisted, his eyes warm with pride and respect. "No—I mean General MacArthur himself. Say, he ain't afraid of nothing."

Against the remonstrations of his Staff MacArthur had insisted on personally leading this "reconnaissance in force" so that he would be on hand to appraise the situation and assume the responsibility personally as to whether they should remain or withdraw. If he stayed he would be able to save many lives, great effort and valuable time. It was one of those rare moments in war which were redolent with destiny.

He calmly surveyed the situation. Japanese by the hundreds

would soon be counter-attacking; they would come streaming over from nearby Manus. The heavy weather robbed him of air support from Kenney, but he held the critical point—he had the airfield. He would stick. He turned to Chase and said: "You've got your teeth in him now. Don't let go." And Chase grinned, and swore that the whole Japanese Army couldn't move him.

MacArthur now turned to his own Senior Naval Officer, Vice Admiral Kinkaid, who was by his side, and ordered reinforcements brought in at full speed. Long before this he had thought out that possibility; the ships were already loaded and on the sea. They'd come up that very night. Soon Custer's immortal Seventh Cavalry, and the famous Twelfth would be coming along with the rest of the Fifth. They'd all fight. MacArthur had grasped the key to the Bismarck Sea, and he proposed to hold it.

Somehow he sensed that the cool fire had gone out of the Japanese here. His men could handle them, even when the odds were five to one against them. "These dismounted Cavalrymen are incomparable Infantry," he pronounced. And that night they proved it when the crazed, wild-minded Nips charged again and again, only to be mowed down by Yank fire—as all men go down when seared by white streams of hot machine-gun bullets.

Fighting went on for days. It was kill, kill, kill. There was nothing else to do with those Japanese fanatics. It took some time, but these horseless Cavalrymen were master craftsmen, and for every twenty Nips killed the Yanks lost but one.

Below, in the jungle islands that fringed the Bismarck and Solomon Seas, more than 150,000 still lived. Death would come slowly to most of them. They would grow gaunt and hollow from hunger and fever and loneliness. They would dream of cherry blossoms in lovely far-away valleys—but they would never see them again.

The communique of the day made clear the great victory:

"This marks a final stage in the great swinging move pivoting on New Guinea which has been the basic purpose of the operations initiated on June 29, 1943, when the Southwest Pacific Area and South Pacific Area were united under General MacArthur's command. The axis of advance has thereby been changed from the north to the west. This relieves our supply line of the constant threat of flank attack which has been present since the beginning of the Papuan Campaign. This line, previously so precariously exposed, is now firmly secured not only by air coverage, but by our own front to which it is perpendicular. The operation has been a delicate one and its final success lays a strategically firm foundation for the future. The enemy's supply lines are definitely and conclusively severed and only a minimum of blockade running, by submarine or individual surface craft, is now possible. In addition to the 20,000 troops trapped in the Solomons, some fifty thousand of the enemy, largely in New Britain and at Rabaul, are now inclosed. Their situation has become precarious and their ultimate fate is certain under blockade, bombardment and the increasing pressure of besieging ground forces. The end of the Bismarck Campaign is now clearly in sight with a minimum of loss to ourselves."

Bear Hug Number Two was ended. MacArthur could now shift his gaze far off to the westward, and a little to the north. There lay his "Holy Grail."

CHAPTER NINE

THE SUDDEN AND SENSATIONAL CAPTURE OF THE ADMIRALTIES and the complete neutralization of the Japanese air threats from the bases at Rabaul and Kavieng, had set matters forward weeks and months in advance of schedule. Nimitz's fleet had been earmarked to assist in the Admiralty operations, but the strike had been made with such complete surprise and daring, that it had not been necessary for MacArthur to call for outside help.

One other factor loomed large in the picture: Nimitz, following his strike into the Marshalls, had descended on the Japanese base at Truk. Heavy, swift task forces, with a number of fast carriers, approached the sea bastion, and hundreds of planes were launched from the flat-tops and hit Truk with irresistible force.

Next Nimitz struck a quick blow at Palau, 800 miles on westward from Truk. Use of these bases by enemy sea and air forces offered a constant threat to MacArthur's forces moving up through the Bismarck Sea, and seriously handicapped any possible move northwestward towards the Philippines.

Both these bases were now partially neutralized for any large-scale offensive action by the Japanese. It was time for MacArthur to plot his next great move on the Long Road back. His sea flanks were temporarily adequately protected, and he might hope for sturdy carrier-based air help from the Central Pacific forces.

It had been his original plan to make this next strike at the Jap base at Hansa Bay, some 120 miles on up the coast from the last American-Australian outpost at Saidor in New Guinea. Part way up the shore line from our base at Saidor, stood Madang, guarded by 5,500 Japanese troops. To the northwest from Madang a motor road led to Hansa Bay. Along this road was probably a full enemy division which could be rushed to meet any attack in this area. Besides this, at Hansa Bay itself were some 10,000 to 15,000 Japanese troops.

This meant that if MacArthur by-passed Madang and struck at Hansa Bay, he would, at best, advance his line a scant 120 miles—and still have to face initially some 15,000 determined Japs. This was not his type of strategy. He always planned to "hit 'em where they ain't"—not to hit them where they were.

On MacArthur's Headquarters staff was an extremely able G-2, or Intelligence head. He was a professional soldier of splendid training and qualifications. Daily he kept MacArthur and his staff supplied with the best available last-minute details and dispositions of the enemy, and estimated with surprising accuracy the strength of the air and ground forces at the various enemy strongholds.

These reports of Charles Willoughby, now a brigadier general, were invaluable to his Chief. MacArthur constantly told his staff: "You cannot fight the enemy unless you know where and what he is."

Further on to the northwest from Hansa Bay, up the Guinea coast, stood the great enemy base of Wewak. Here it was estimated there were not less than 16,000 Japanese troops. MacArthur might hit this advanced point and by-pass both Madang and Hansa Bay, but he would be hitting them where they were, not where "they ain't." It would be deadly and costly and he was utterly opposed to a bloody frontal assault when possible to avoid it.

Some 200 miles further on to the west of Wewak was the base

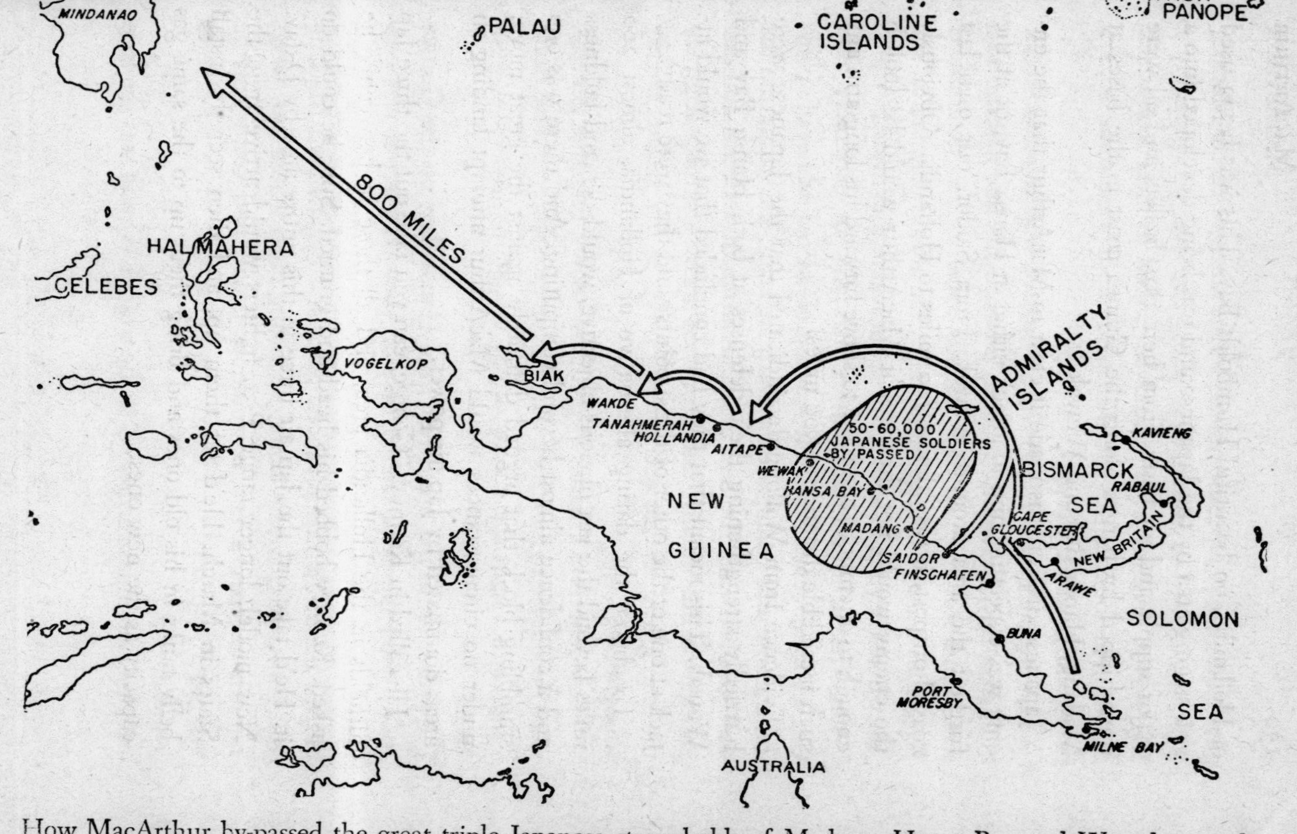

How MacArthur by-passed the great triple Japanese strongholds of Madang, Hansa Bay and Wewak to make a 750-mile forward pass.

of Hollandia, on beautiful Humboldt Bay. This was being used as a staging area by the Japanese and was being developed into a major supply and air base. From here rice, bullets and oil were transshipped by barges along the Guinea coast to the bases at Madang, Hansa Bay and Wewak.

Japanese dispositions made it clear to MacArthur that the enemy was expecting him to attack either at Hansa Bay, or at the furthest the area around Wewak. From Saidor, our own last coastal outpost, it was almost 500 miles to Hollandia. Obviously the enemy would not dream that MacArthur would be foolish enough to attempt at one blow to shove forward his long arm any such incredible distance as 500 miles.

Evidence from Willoughby indicated that the Japanese were hurriedly strengthening their defenses at both Hansa Bay and Wewak. This meant that they had concluded that we would attack at one or the other of these points—and they were ready.

To choose the daring alternative of Hollandia, almost 200 miles beyond the last obvious objective, would demand boldness and a confidence almost beyond computing. And there was one stumbling block that argued definitely against the great move; under no circumstances would MacArthur attempt landing in areas dominated by Jap air power.

He called in Kenney. "George, can you take out the three Jap airfields in the Hollandia area, and all those in between?" he asked. Kenney bobbed his head and grinned. Sure he could do it. He'd take out the Jap air force in this entire area by D-day. New model, longer range P-39 fighters would arrive from the States in March. He'd set them up, and then secretly install belly tanks in his old ones and bring them up to the same gas capacity as the new ones.

With the cunning of a fox, Kenney held his fire until he was ready. Carefully he had stopped fighters from flying further than Tadji, so that the Nips would believe he could not send his bombers by daylight to Hollandia, for lack of fighter cover. Without this protection it was dangerous and suicidal to send out bombers in the daytime. And night bombings at best were unsatisfactory in these uncharted reaches where fogs and heavy weather might spring up as unannounced as tiny whirlwinds on dusty country roads.

Kenney and his two head hatchet men, Major General Whitehead, and the Fifth Air Force Chief of Staff, Colonel Marion Cooper—soon to be made a "B. G."—licked their chops in anticipation. They were certain that they would catch the Nips wide open as a barn door. They would gamble their lives that these Japs in Hollandia had not the slightest fear of air attack, because they were certain we had no fighters that could fly more than two-thirds the distance. But they underestimated the imagination and determined purposefulness of these relentless Americans.

MacArthur's purpose was breath-taking. He would by-pass some 60,000 Japanese troops ready and waiting for him on the road to Hollandia; he would pin them down by feints and deceptions, he would make a great surprise attack on this final base—and thus in one master stroke advance his front almost five hundred miles. Once Hollandia was in his hands, he could rapidly build a great land, sea and air base there, while those 60,000 fanatical Nips, left high and dry, could slowly starve to death.

He would have them in a great loop of envelopment, this 18th Japanese Army, just as he had trapped the 17th Japanese Army in similar loops in the Solomons and New Britain. These were the two armies, a quarter of a million strong, originally destined to invade Australia. He would then have them isolated with their ultimate destruction certain.

With his decision made, his next move was to secure the help of the great Central Pacific Fleet. Nimitz flew to MacArthur's Headquarters. Rear Admiral Barbey, able commander of MacArthur's Seventh Amphibious Fleet, would have to have additional amphibious equipment, supply and troop ships, extra cruisers and destroyers, and at least a handful of the small but effective Escort Carriers. Besides this, there would have to be covering forces to guard the right flank against any sudden Japanese sea attack, and fast carriers to knock out Japanese airfields further on west—and then cover the actual landings on the Guinea coast.

Kenney's bombers unquestionably would be able to destroy Japanese airpower at the Hollandia fields before the invasion began, but the moment the landings started the air protection would have to come from the navy carriers; it would be impossible for his fighters to hover long enough over the target to cover a landing.

Nimitz wholeheartedly agreed to furnish ample naval vessels and carrier-based air support. He would cooperate to the fullest extent. The two men saw eye to eye, and their personal meeting was to be of inestimable value. They would each help the other in the coming joint missions. They had a single objective—the quick and complete defeat of Japan.

MacArthur had plans prepared to "lift" not only an army of 50,000 men but, as well, a great city with its stores, garages, hospitals, power plants, fire departments, post office and a hundred and one items of daily need. The troops would be gathered at Goodenough Island and at another great base. The armada would move in three groups to the Admiralties, and there at dawn of April 20, join together and openly head northwest. Japanese reconnaissance planes, and their own intelligence agencies, would probably discover the armada moving northwest and would decide it was headed for Palau. But there would be a quick "cut back" to the New Guinea coast, blissfully unprepared and unsuspecting.

Altogether more than three hundred ships of one kind or another were required for the operation—as well as the task forces and swift carriers that Nimitz would send to guard the right flank and make the necessary last-minute air strikes and coverings. Considering distance and numbers involved, it would be unprecedented. There would be just enough to do the job—and not a man or ship more than necessary to make the vast operation secure.

MacArthur was now ready for Kenney to do his big job. For days Kenney had been plastering the intervening bases at Madang, Hansa Bay and Wewak. All three had been knocked out, and for the time being their deadly counter air threat completely removed. (Turn back to map on page 149.)

Not a single American bomber or fighter had ventured beyond Tadji in the daytime, which inspired the belief in Jap minds that they were safe beyond that point. Obviously it was impossible to reach there, so the Japanese had boldly been flying their precious aircraft into Hollandia to be sent on southward when the battered fields were repaired, or when the expected attack on Hansa Bay or Wewak came.

At dawn on March 30th our air force struck Hollandia with the fury of a Kansas cyclone. Ninety heavies, each carrying 52 clusters of fragmentation bombs, cut to pieces more than a hundred Japanese planes. The following day they struck again, but this time the ships carried 1,000-pound bombs as well as "frags"—and when it was over 1,300 tons of bombs had ripped to ribbons the shore installations, where landings would be made. On April 3rd they let loose a low-level attack of deadly B-25's with their eight 50-caliber guns. Photographs showed that in the three attacks the Japs had a total of 351 planes either destroyed or rendered useless—and later actual count proved that, including those shot down in combat, they had destroyed a Jap air force of 450 planes. It was the greatest air murder in history.

The airmen continued to pound the three fields until they looked like broken sieves. Quickly thousands of Japanese laborers and ground crews filled in the craters—only to have the bombers return and undo all their work.

Meanwhile the plans for the ground forces were being coordinated. Lieut. General Bob Eichelberger, one of the heroes of the terrible Buna campaign, was given a Corps made up of most of the units of the 24th and 41st U. S. Infantry Divisions—along with such special artillery and auxiliary troops as were needed. His job would be to capture Hollandia and the tiny port of Tanahmerah, 30 miles west of Hollandia—then push through from both points and double-envelop the three airfields that lay some fifteen miles back from the coast. These strips were protected by the rain forests and the almost impassable Cyclops Mountains.

To the eastward 120 miles from Hollandia, was the port and airfield of Aitape. Lieut. General Walter Krueger, Commander of the 6th Army, reserved one regimental team from the 41st Division for the capture of this thinly-held but important Jap airfield, and gave the command to an excellent soldier, Brigadier General Gene Doe.

There would be a definite feint made at Hansa Bay on the

morning the actual attacks were to be launched more than 300 miles beyond. If everything worked out smoothly—and luckily—the entire triple operations would come off in complete surprise and with a minimum loss of American life. That was the "MacArthur touch."

* * * *

In all the history of seafaring there probably has never been a picture more majestic than the vista of this vast armada sweeping west from the Admiralties. It had assembled here during the night of April 19–20, and when dawn broke there spread out before the eyes of 50,000 ship-borne soldiers and thousands of sailors a whole horizon filled with vessels bound for the war.

They moved ahead in a great circle, ten miles across. Swift destroyers rode the outer fringes, as scouts in the Indian days used to ride the circle of the covered wagons, bound for the distant, unknown West. Each of the three groups that would make the triple landings marched in columns within the great circle. On a destroyer far ahead rode tough, able Walter Krueger. In the position of control, came Admiral Barbey's flagship, likewise a swift and proud destroyer. Aboard was Lieut. General Eichelberger, Commander of the two most important operations, and the fabulous Colonel Earickson, Air coordinator of Nimitz's flattops and the ground forces.

Off to the right and left, in the inner line of guards, came American and Australian cruisers. On one cruiser that flew the Stars and Stripes rode the man who would be held responsible for the entire campaign. There must be no failure.

He wore his forage cap as always in battle—the one with the battered gold embroidery around it. No steel helmet for him!

Thousands of soldiers would soon be thrilled by the sight of it. For he was going ashore with his beloved soldiers—to share their danger and their victory or defeat. Before night fell on the great day of April 22nd, he was to visit two of the beaches, and on the following day he would go ashore at Aitape, 120 miles back down the coast.

Ceaselessly those destroyer outriders covered the horizon. No enemy sub dared try to penetrate the circle. But always there was the possibility of sudden air attacks from Japanese dive and torpedo bombers. Escort carriers, trailing the western group, but well within the circle, sent up their fighters, and all through the lazy, blue days they watched over the great armada.

Far to the northward a mighty task force with the deadliest and swiftest battle wagons of America's beautiful new Battle Fleet—along with the fast carriers and their cruiser and destroyer escorts—rode the ranges of the distant seas. They prayed they might lure the Japanese fleet from its new bases in Mindanao and Singapore. They asked only for a whack at it—a part of it, or all of it. They were bold and cocky and utterly confident.

On April 21st—D minus one day—hundreds of American fighters and dive bombers left their carriers and searched out the enemy air bases, three, four hundred miles on up the rugged Dutch Guinea coast. Kenney was not to attack the Hollandia bases after the morning of this day; the carriers' bombers would give the three fields their final shellacking.

Early on the morning of D day the three groups of the great armada executed the "cut back" and each group headed straight for its separate mission. Towards Aitape the escort carriers went with the vessels they were guarding. They would attend to the preliminary beach-bombing there.

For the Hollandia and the Tanahmerah landings, air protection would come from the fast carriers of the task forces. There must be no fumbling. Every possibility had been studied and solved. No single detail was missing.

At 6:20—H hour minus 75 minutes—the ships of war that had accompanied the convoys opened their preliminary bombardments. Shells streaked through the gray dawn skies—shrieked and flashed, carrying their death and destruction.

Again the surprise was complete and unmeetable. The few Japanese troops at each of the landing beaches fled in terror and helplessness. They abandoned guns, cannon, mortars, vast supplies of food and equipment—and the rain forests and green mountains of New Guinea swallowed them up.

At Hollandia alone there were accumulated supplies that would have lasted 10,000 Japanese troops for six months. Two or three days before the landings, Kenney's bombers had started a fire among these supplies, and the Japanese had been unable to put it out completely. On the beaches nearby long, lean, green-splotched LST's pushed straight onto the sand, opened wide their doors, and out rode trucks piled high with supplies. By nightfall thousands of tons of foodstuffs, shells and equipment had been piled up there on the narrow beaches.

The fires in the Japanese supply dumps were burning only a little now, but the tiny flame was a living red signal that could be seen miles away across the sky. At 7:40 that first night, while thousands of tired men were digging their slit trenches, preparing their gun mounts and setting up camp on nearby Pancake Hill, an unknown raider swooped down through the gathering twilight. He had followed that beacon of fire that licked the night with its bright, red tongue.

Carefully he swung down the beach and dropped his stick of eight 100-pound bombs. Four of them hit squarely in the midst of the inflammable boxes, oil drums and the several thousand tons of stores that had been piled up on the beach that day. The explosions tossed his light bomber high in the blazing skies. It righted and he sped through the darkness back to his base. The strike caused considerable damage but interfered only to the slightest degree with the advance towards the air strips far to the rear. Sweating, weary doughboys slithered through the red mud of Pancake Hill, and slogged over the trail that led from the tiny landing at Pim towards the air strips fifteen miles away. At the same time other tired, thirsty and worn foot sloggers, thirty miles on down the coast at Tanahmerah, pushed their way up the narrow, steep track that had been cut by hand out of the timbered sides of the green mountains. Tropical trees, festooned with moss and vines, hung over the narrow, muddy trail. The humid, sticky heat, clinging to the soggy, slippery track, was as enervating and exhausting as the miasmic mists that lie endlessly in the rain forests and weird green jungles of this island continent.

The mountain trails led over the foothills of the Cyclops Mountains, down to the three airfields. It was a strange and exciting race that was now taking place between the advancing battalions of Horace Fuller's 41st Infantry Division, based at Hollandia, and the front units of Fred Irving's 24th Division operating over the mountains from the beaches of Tanahmerah. In the end, after three days' struggle against a nature that was more stubborn and difficult than the Japanese resistance, the honors were divided almost equally between the two divisions. Each had won toeholds on the airstrips, and each had helped equally in the great victory.

Two days later our fighters were landing on the strips the bulldozers had leveled off; in a few days more the heavy bombers were dropping in. The Bomber Line had been advanced 500 miles. And here in the coconut plantations and jungle a great advance base was already building. Before long tens of thousands of troops, millions of pounds of supplies and equipment—a vast army-in-being—would be centered here.

The advancing Bomber Line would coincide with the advancing Staging Area. Hollandia, the sleepy little Dutch native village long forgotten and neglected, would mushroom into a vivid, busy port, with hundreds of ships riding lazily in its beautiful harbor. Daring deeds would be mounted here, and from its sandy shores great argosies of war would embark.

Within a month after that strange and devastating blaze on the beaches the first of these new advancing arms of steel would shoot out from Hollandia. From those newly captured fields behind the Cyclops, our bombers and fighters would first blast to bits the remaining airstrips on the head of the great setting buzzard of New Guinea.

Suddenly at dawn on May 17th ships would emerge from the dark horizon—ships bearing grim, brave boys from far-away homes. They would grab another air base at Wakde. And ten days later MacArthur would shoot his long arm around the neck of the Guinea buzzard and swoop down on Biak Island in Geevlink Bay.

These two jumps alone would take him 350 miles nearer his dreams—his lovely but prostrate Philippines. He would never stop to rest until he reached their shores and made good his vows of liberation. The dead, the cruelly starved and ravaged prisoners of Bataan and Corregidor, of Manila and a hundred native barrios—all would in the end be avenged.

* * * *

It would be a grave error to think that these brilliant victories which we have won at such small cost can continue indefinitely. We have actually punctured only the outer perimeter of the Japanese defense.

The Japanese are already rushing new defenses for an interior perimeter, where enemy supply lines will be shorter and more secure. The Japanese still have their battle fleet—slightly out of kilter though it may be. But it remains still a deadly striking weapon. Our own new beautiful fleet is more powerful than is this enemy fleet, but the Pacific is a sea of vast distances—and there are times when our fleet must be beyond supporting distance. At these times of danger MacArthur's amphibious operations become vulnerable.

His land-based air is effective against the enemy fleet within range—but should the enemy fleet come in under a cold weather front then our bombers could not find it—and our supply ships and amphibious craft would be absolutely helpless. As a consequence, unless MacArthur's operations are supported by the Central Pacific Fleet—over which he has no command whatsoever—his moves forward are characterized by great risks. For all his strategic victories he is forced to be a cautious man. Now and again he will take long chances, as in his magnificent surprise swoops on the Admiralties. There are times when every commander must take these chances.

Without adequate naval support MacArthur is forced to accept these risks. It is his sure touch, his consummate military genius, that has brought him victory up to this time.

He is on the way back. But it is a long road, with disaster lurking at a hundred turns. Japan is definitely on the defensive, but the war is still to be won. We have a fine and flowing start—but it is still only a beginning.

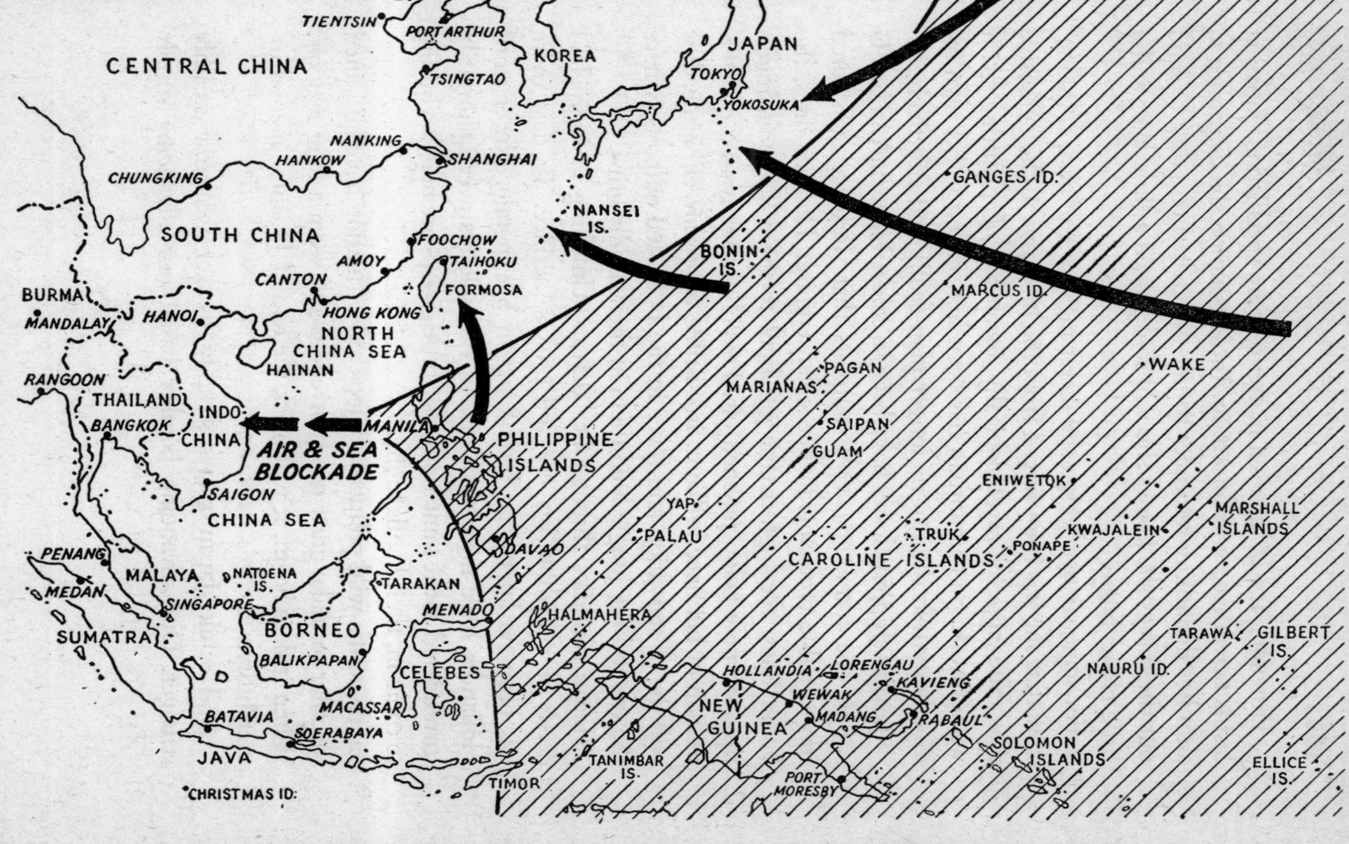

An estimate of the U. S. advances in the Pacific once the Philippines are captured.

How long it will take is a matter of pure speculation. Japan at last is bewildered and uncertain. In desperation she continues to ship her dwindling resources to her threatened outposts; to send out the things she knows she will sorely need a little later and a little closer home.

For some strange reason she seems incapable of clear thinking, now that she has been forced from the offensive to the defensive role. She appears psychologically incapable of planning great withdrawals. So gargantuan has been her conceit in her own invincibility that she can no longer plan coolly and effectively.

Japan's shipping losses have been so colossal that she can barely supply the former powerful outposts that she once considered impregnable protectors of her stolen empire. The rice lines, the bullet lines, the high octane gas lines to these far-flung fingertips, are now being pinched off. Possibly as many as a quarter-million of her once brilliant, irresistible troops are either dead or will die of starvation and fever in the by-passed outposts, where the sea and the jungle hold them in their deadly grips.

Japan muddles through her defeats, clutching at individual deeds of incredible bravery and useless sacrifice. To date there has been no large-scale breakdown in her morale. Never until Hollandia have more than one or two soldiers ever voluntarily surrendered at the same time. But little groups are now beginning to come in, their hands high above their heads. Pride, fear, propaganda, and a wild politico-religious indoctrination have all joined together to make great mass surrender still seem a long way off. When it does begin, it will mark the end of Japanese mental invincibility.

And while Japan grows steadily weaker we grow steadily stronger. Our advancing bomber bases, our advancing supply bases and staging areas; our slowly increasing land and sea and air power, make certain there will be daring operations in the future.

A band of American undersea heroes has struck them heavily. Brave, tough, self-sufficient subs have sunk not less than 700 of their supply ships. Our air force and swift destroyers and packs of those hungry, roving wolves of the sea—the daring PT-boats—have accounted for hundreds of others. It is Japan now that has little with which to do so much.

Leaders, once so cocksure and intolerable, have been guilty of the prime military crime of over-extending themselves. They had not dreamed that America could shake herself sufficiently free from the disaster of Pearl Harbor and her European commitments, and so quickly be able to gird up her loins and build incredible fleets and armies, and planes almost beyond count.

Only a tiny fraction of this great stream of production was to be allocated to the far Western Pacific—but the genius of a single man was largely to compensate for this holding back, for one cause or another, of the matériel and men of war.

Japan, still extended over a front more than 3,000 miles long, cannot adequately defend every point and base. With a deadly scientific approach, MacArthur goes about his business of "hittin' 'em where they ain't"—by-passing the strong points and Japanese concentrations and then suddenly leaping far ahead at some lightly-held strategic area.

After each operation he revalues, rediagnoses the enemy's dispositions and strengths. Once he gains this knowledge, he plans and strikes with deadly sureness. Within his means, he can feint, parry, shift his attack, then strike at the time and place of his own choosing.

He will undertake no move unless it is clear that his losses will be light. No victory is, in his eyes, worth a great cost in human life. He will have no part in slaughter.

It is an astounding fact that his total losses in the first two years of fighting, after he took command in Australia, have been fewer killed in action than America lost in the single operation for the beaches of Anzio.

For here in the distant and long neglected far Western Pacific, MacArthur has constantly risen to the impossible. He has won despite everything. He would not be intimidated, nor could his moral courage be broken.

He remained the free mind that refused to be chained or slowed down. He could look the world squarely in the eye and honestly say that he had been tempted neither by stars on his shoulder nor ribbons on his chest, to do things that were not good and true for his country.

The faith that had let John J. Pershing, noble old warrior, stand true and worthy on the battlefields of France when wavering Allies and timid Washington urged him to give up control of his precious American army—this same faith was to sustain MacArthur. No amount of badgering and bullying, of threatening and intimidating, could force John J. Pershing to break up his armies and put his country completely at the mercy of the judgment and integrity of outside forces. To do so would have lost us the invaluable, the irrecoverable power of decision. It would have loosed the grip—and American dignity and sovereignty would have fallen like dead bits of paper through the fingers.

Clear as crystal have been the decisions of this man MacArthur. He has fought the good fight for his country and for the men who tried so hard and so long in battered Corregidor and Bataan.

He has something to fight with now—although it is far from a sufficiency. Yet by an uncanny sense of the fitness of things, he is able to force his will as and where he chooses against a frightened and bewildered enemy. His objective will always be decisive. No outside influences can ever force him to waste men and means and time on indecisive objectives.

He will never lose this superiority of will—this final decisive weapon of war. He will slowly impose his will on first this particular point of contact, then on that, and on the others to follow after.

He will stride straight across the seas and islands until his feet touch the land of the Philippines.

Here lies the fulfilment of his solemn vows. Here lies the key to a final Pacific victory.

CHAPTER TEN

MacARTHUR HAD MADE A STUBBORN FIGHT IN THE PHILIPpines during those tragic December days of 1941, and in the months that followed. His resistance had knocked the Japanese war machine completely off center.

The block he set on the road southward had held up not less than 200,000 Japanese troops, 1,000 planes and a great armada of troop, supply, and warships. Instead of snuffing out the totally inadequate defense forces in Luzon, as the Japanese High Command believed they could do, they were forced to settle down to a dreary and expensive time-consuming operation.

They still had large and powerful forces to carry on their drives down through Singapore, Burma and the Netherlands East Indies, but the delicate schedule of their over-all plan of sudden conquest was knocked off balance. The months of delay caused by MacArthur's strategy and timing, unquestionably saved both India and Australia from being overrun in these early mad rushes.

The effort of checking and blocking the southern and western movement, and the resultant failure of the Japanese to get new power drives going in time to overwhelm these two great continents, cannot be overestimated. It meant that neither India nor Australia would be cut off from at least some American help. It gave the Allies great bases for future operations. It saved the whole South Pacific and much of southeastern Asia.

Had India gone, the last road into China—the final link—would have been broken. It is to be doubted if China under these lonely and isolated circumstances would have long remained in the war. And if China had collapsed, the effect on all this part of the world would have been catastrophic.

It was the fight that MacArthur and his men—and the loyal people of the Philippines—put up that was to stop the tide of disaster. It was largely due to the character and integrity of this one man that the 60,000 native soldiers of the Philippines Army in Luzon fought so stubbornly and courageously. And it is doubtful if any one else could have inspired his Regulars, both American and natives, to such gallantry. Certainly no one else could have fought the lost cause with more consummate tactical and strategical skill.

MacArthur had long been a legendary figure throughout all the scattered islands. In every nook and corner there were Filipino youth who had been called into the Philippine Army, that had been the beloved child of MacArthur's talent and determination. For six years he had been slowly building it up, and had he had four years more, and the proper funds and military assistance from America, he would have had a superb defense force.

As it was, Filipinos, green and untrained in working in any organization larger than companies, fought hard, once the first shock of battle swept over them. They died willingly—and they died just as much for MacArthur as they did for their own country. The two were entwined in their hearts.

* * * *

Two years almost to a day after MacArthur was ordered by the President of the United States to go to Australia, a Filipino officer escaped from the Islands and made his way to General

Headquarters in Australia. He asked to be taken to General MacArthur.

The tall soldier, with the four tiny stars on the collar of his khaki shirt gleaming like his dark eyes, listened carefully while the refugee told his story. . . .

In one of the elementary schools in Manila the teacher had been ordered by a Japanese inspector to have the pictures of President Quezon and General MacArthur, that were stamped on the cover of one of the textbooks, pasted over with black paper. One by one the children brought their books for inspection to the teacher with the Japanese agent sitting by his side. One little boy laid down his book. But there was no paper pasted over the picture.

The boy was told that he must do it at once. He did not answer, but stood quietly awaiting his punishment. The Japanese official blustered and threatened. The little boy made no move. Over and over again he refused.

Then the Japanese inspector ordered the teacher to deface the pictures of the two heroes. The teacher refused; he had gained new courage from his pupil. The Japanese demanded he carry out the orders immediately. Stubbornly he refused. The Japanese then had him arrested, and he was carted off to some unknown fate.

MacArthur, deeply touched, could only whisper, "Brave boy."

* * *

Then the Filipino refugee told a second story. . . .

In Manila the Japanese had suggested that it would be well to have various groups of citizens assemble at a series of meetings, where they could have it explained to them that the Americans had made no effort to send them help, and that they had deserted them forever. At the first meeting held, the native Quisling who conducted the meeting said, "We must all work with the Japanese now—for MacArthur will never return to us."

When the speaker had finished there was complete silence. Not a man applauded. Then in the awesome moment when even the Japanese official present did not quite know what to do, an elderly, poorly dressed Filipino arose in the rear of the hall.

Tears were streaming down his face as he shouted, "You lie! You lie! He told us he would return and he WILL return!"

The General could not restrain his emotion as he heard the story. To those accustomed to his usual dignified composure, it was a revelation.

"Every Filipino waits for you, sir," the native officer went on, his voice trembling with his own pent-up grief and pain. "We will fight only for you. . . . It is you we want. . . ."

Then he broke down and sobbed.

* * * *

In a strange way the Philippines are not only the key to victory over the Japanese, but they are the key to a friendly, just solution of the great racial, nationalistic and social problems of the billion peoples of Asia.

Between the islands and the mainland of Asia lies the South China Sea, roughly some seven hundred miles wide. It is the sea road that runs straight to Japan from the rich reservoirs of stolen war materials in Malaya and the Dutch East Indies. Up this sea road come the oil and rubber, copper, manganese and chrome, quinine and rice, and a score and more raw materials vital to the Japanese war economy. It is the only short and feasible road.

Once this sea lane is cut, Japan will be deprived of the flow of these needed supplies. She will have only her reserves to fall back on. She will be cut off, isolated, marooned. She will immediately be on the defensive—and slowly into the consciousness of her people will come the horrible knowledge that their warlords and military priests have deceived them and their sacred Emperor. They will face humiliation and eventually defeat from that moment on.

Once the United States has gained strong footholds in the Philippines, our bombers, submarines and swift surface craft will cut these Japanese supply lines, as surely as night follows day. The strategic Chinese coastal cities and strongholds now in Japanese hands will crumple one by one. The Chinese will take care of that matter. The sun will begin to set over the arrogant Japanese Empire.

Those are the reasons why MacArthur's determination to retake the Philippines at the earliest possible moment, is so sound and imperative. Once Philippine air and naval bases are in our hands, the doom of Japan is not only assured, but it will be hastened.

* * * *

The sturdy waiting of the Philippine people for MacArthur's return is a beautiful commentary on what decent relationship between two peoples, sealed over a long period of time, can do. Here more than forty years of mutual respect, of carrying out of pledges and promises, of a thousand proofs of honesty and integrity, now come to their full fruition.

Here, for the first time in the history of conquest and imperialism, people of one race and color have been treated as full and proud equals by an outside race. Here for the first time liberties and independence promised have unreservedly been given. The United States wanted no gain or loot from the Islands. She wanted only to be generous and fair. Douglas MacArthur's father had been one of the leaders of the little band of fine, long-visioned, freedom-loving American officials and army officers who laid out the fundamental precepts of ultimate independence.

It was this fair treatment that made the Filipinos ready to fight and die proudly under the twin flags, when the moment of decision and trial came. It is the reason seventeen million Filipinos fervently pray for the return of MacArthur and his Americans.

For in these rich and lovely Islands the way has been found for two peoples to live and prosper together. Only here has the way been found. And until the remaining billion of Asiatics and their warlords work out together some such road to understanding, and mutual aid and independence, there can be no final peace in the Orient.

The keystone of Japan's dream of Asiatic conquest and cooperation was nothing short of arousing these billion Orientals to a holy war against the white man. Had China accepted this idea, Asia would have been lost beyond the slightest doubt. Nothing could have stopped the spread of Japanese-inspired resentment and revenge.

China, fortunately, mistrusted and feared the Japanese. She held fast to her resentment against Japan, and to her determination to run her own affairs. Japan, determined and relentless, finally bogged down in the vast distances and inertia of China. To pursue her ambitions she was forced to use up much of her energy and resources. She continues to waste them in her stubborn attempts to conquer China.

China trusts only the United States. We have played reasonably fair with her. The same holds true for the other lands and peoples of the Oriental world. The example that American-Philippine happy relationship has set has been both an irritant and an inspiration to the billion natives scattered throughout the Western Pacific and the Indian Ocean.

And so it is that the Philippines are the key to all hopes and plans for a decent, lasting peace in this distant world. It is necessary for the long tomorrow that Philippine independence be restored and given new life. Only by this can victory come and peace be assured.

It was a holy cause that MacArthur embarked on when he pledged his sacred honor that he would return to the Islands and set them free.

And the Way Back may not be as long or as expensive as the world fears it will be.

EPILOGUE

THE BRILLIANT HOLLANDIA OPERATION WAS OVER, AND MacArthur was at his sprawling bungalow in Port Moresby when I called to say goodbye to him late in May. We talked long and of many things.

We had been old and close friends for years. I can still recall vividly my first meeting with him. It was in the early summer of 1918 on the Western Front, and he had just returned from one of those desperate raids which were a thrilling inspiration to all who saw them. He was wearing an old black West Point sweater. A machine-gun bullet had cut the threads of the left arm and it was ravelling. I asked him then: "When did Brigadier Generals become expendable?"

He answered grimly that there were times when even general officers had to become platoon leaders. This moment was one of them, and young Douglas MacArthur had gladly taken up the challenge. He had then the same exalted lift from battle and danger as he has to this day. A look comes into his eyes when danger closes in on him that no one can ever forget, once it is seen. I saw it more than once in France—and 26 years later on the hot beaches of Guinea I was again to mark it. It stamps the exaltation that comes to the true soldier in battle.

In that First World War MacArthur was the youngest Commander on the line; now he is the oldest. Seventeen years and more he has served in foreign lands, far from his country's shores; a longer time than any other general officer in America, I believe.

His services abroad and at home have given him experience

and wisdom. He inherited a third quality that all great commanders must have—integrity.

A great commander's will to win is not an easy matter to understand or to explain. Yet no real victories are won without it. It might be called "an accumulation of determinations." A commander must make up his mind to pursue a certain course, attain a certain objective—and then let nothing in Heaven or earth shake him from his decision.

It must have the quality and force of a great spiritual vow. Such mighty determinations cannot be casually made or quickly carried through. They call for the stubborn spiritual quality and power of a true religious leader. They are based on sincerity, character, moral courage—and they all add up to this unbreakable will to win.

In this man there is deep and abiding spiritual fiber. Time and again he has shown the strength of his religious background. His philosophy is simple and direct. "I have utter and complete confidence in a merciful God," he has said. "And God helps those who help themselves." It is the final proof of the sincerity of his character. Without it he could never have touched the inner springs of the millions of trusting Filipinos. Without it he could never have won and held the respect and love of the Australian people and their leaders.

It has made him steadfast and stalwart. In his mind true religion inspires and creates an invincible force for stirring deeds. Leaders have had it throughout the ages. It is the indivisible urge that makes men go to their death—even when there is fear.

In his own words, "More men have died in the name of God than for any other cause." Every real leader has inspired his men with a sublime spiritual force.

It has been this abiding spiritual force within MacArthur

which has sustained him. Throughout his desperate struggles, in spite of great odds and handicaps that at times have deliberately been placed against him, he has never wavered.

His own complete confidence in his men is a living part of his faith. He has pride in them and in their attainments. His Orders of the Day resound with their praises. He demands that they be given full justice and that their self-respect be maintained. He has tolerance and understanding of their problems.

At heart he is a shy man. His necessary aloofness and austerity have been wrongly interpreted to be merely showmanship. Never for a moment does he step out of character.

Human suffering touches him to the quick. Always he demands of his planners that no single American boy be sacrificed needlessly. If there is the slightest suspicion in his mind that an advance might cost heavily he invariably switches objectives or softens resistance by heavy bombings. The lives of his soldiers are precious, even sacred to him.

His proud and simple Americanism is as clear and profound as his great soldierly qualities. He has said to me more than once: "I have been a professional soldier for more than forty years—but I have been an American citizen all my life."

He is just that—a "soldier-citizen." He is zealous of his country's right; of her right to control her own destinies in both peace and war.

He believes above all else that America must hold fast to her freedom and her sovereignty. She must help the world—but above all she must make herself strong and secure.

She must trust herself, and realize that only Americans can loyally plot the course of her future. She must hold fast the direction of her own affairs—of her part in the war, and in the peace to come.

In this man is the uncompromising will to win, and the character and integrity to lead his country to ultimate victory on the battlefields of the world. The respect of the world is his. Men and nations know that when others may fail they can always turn to him for leadership and victory.

The hour was late, and a cloud had drifted over the moon. A cooling south wind was blowing gently across the winding hills and green valleys of this far-away and lonely tropical port in New Guinea.

It was a strange world for an American to be fighting in and for. But only by so doing could his beloved country remain safe and free.

* * * *

In a few short months after these final words are written Douglas MacArthur will have his feet well planted in great Mindanao Island. And a few short months after that he will triumphantly enter Manila—and with his own hands raise on the battered Rock and on deathless Bataan the Stars and Stripes, soiled and besmirked by strutting Japanese.

By his side will be a tired and worn man, but a man of unconquered spirit and determination—Manuel Quezon. MacArthur had pledged his sacred honor that he would return, and that, if still alive, he would bring back with him the beloved Philippine President. That he will do.

It will be a great day for Americans—a day that will live alongside our most honored national memory days. It will be a great day, too, for Filipinos.

And it will be a great day for Douglas MacArthur.

THE END

INDEX